MESSIAH BEN JOSEPH

*A Type in both Jewish
and Christian Traditions*

MESSIAH BEN JOSEPH

*A Type in both Jewish
and Christian Traditions*

Jan Å. Sigvartsen

GlossaHouse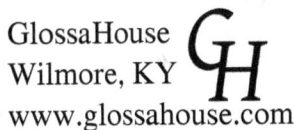
Wilmore, KY
www.glossahouse.com

MESSIAH BEN JOSEPH
A TYPE IN BOTH JEWISH AND CHRISTIAN TRADITIONS

© GlossaHouse, LLC, 2018

All rights reserved. No part of this book may be reproduced or transmitted in any form or by any means, electronic or mechanical, including photocopying or recording, or by means of any information storage or retrieval system, except as may be expressly permitted by the 1976 Copyright Act or in writing from the publisher. Requests for permission should be addressed in writing to the following:

GlossaHouse, LLC
110 Callis Circle
Wilmore, KY 40309
www.GlossaHouse.com

Messiah Ben Joseph
A Type in both Jewish and Christian Traditions

Sigvartsen, Jan Å.
      xxii, 138 p. 22.86 cm. — (GlossaHouse monograph series:
            studies in texts & language; vol. 1)
Includes bibliographical references and indexes.
Library of Congress Control Number: 2018930612
ISBN 9781942697558 (hardback)
ISBN 9781942697435 (paperback)

1. Bible. Genesis, XLIX, 22-26–Criticism, interpretation, etc.
2. Messiah–Biblical teaching. 3. Messiah–Judaism. 4. Typology (Theology)
5. Joseph (Son of Jacob) I. Title. II. Series.

BS680.M4 S53 2018   232/.12

The English and Greek fonts used to create this work are available from www.linguistsoftware.com/lgku.htm
Interior design by Jan Å. Sigvartsen and Fredrick J. Long
Cover design by T. Michael W. Halcomb

GlossaHouse Monograph Series: Studies in Texts & Language

Volume 1

Series Editors

T. Michael W. Halcomb

Fredrick J. Long

Volume Editor

Fredrick J. Long

GlossaHouse Monograph Series:
Studies in Texts & Language

The goal of the GlossaHouse Monograph Series is to facilitate the creation and publication of innovative, affordable, and accessible scholarly resources, whether print or digital, that advance research in the areas of both ancient and modern texts and languages.

Dedication

For Grethe Lill and Torbjørn Sigvartsen.

Contents

LIST OF ILLUSTRATIONS	xiii
LIST OF TABLES	xiv
LISTS OF ABBREVIATIONS	xv
INTRODUCTION	1
1. HISTORY OF INTERPRETATION	4
Inner-Biblical Interpretation	6
Early Jewish Interpretation (Scribal Exegesis before 70 CE)	7
Septuagint	7
Extra-Canonical Writings	8
Pseudepigraphic Writings	9
Testament of the Twelve Patriarchs	10
The Lamb of God	16
Joseph and Asenath	19
3 Enoch	22
Later Jewish Interpretation (Rabbinic Judaism)	23
Talmud	24
Midrashim	27
Pesiqta Rabbati	29
Apocalyptic Midrashim	31
Medieval Jewish Literature	33
Sa'adiah ben Yoseph Gaon (892-942 CE)	33
Shlomo Yitzchaki (1040-1105 CE)	34
Avraham ben Meir Ibn Ezra (1089-1167 CE)	35
David Kimhi (1160-1235 CE)	37
Moses ben Nachman (1194-1270 CE)	37
Moshe ben Shem-Tov (c. 1240-1305 CE)	38
Isaac ben Judah Abravanel (1437-1508 CE)	39
Moses Alshech (1508-1593 CE)	39
Bacharach, Naphtali Ben Jacob Elchanan	40
The Figure of Joseph in Jewish Traditions	41
Early Christian Period	41
The Enlightenment/Historical Critical Method	43
Summary	43

2. TRANSLATION AND NOTES ON THE JOSEPH ORACLE	46
A Possible Translation	46
Literary Analysis	47
Contextual Analysis	51
The Immediate Context	51
Outline of the Joseph Narrative	53
Literary Pattern of the Pentateuch and the Joseph Story	56
"In the Last Days"	60
3. MESSIANIC/ESCHATOLOGICAL IMPLICATIONS OF THE JOSEPH ORACLE	64
The Messianic Aspects	64
The Suffering Joseph	65
The Loyal and Protected Joseph	66
The Divine Joseph	67
The Blessed Joseph	68
The Royal Joseph	69
The Relationship between Judah and Joseph	73
The Blessings of Judah, Joseph and the Patriarchs Compared	74
Joseph, the Rightful Heir	75
What about the Seed?	78
The Eschatological Aspect	80
Joseph as an Illustration, Type, or Prophecy?	80
Typological Indicator	82
Jesus, the Antitypical Joseph	83
Structure of the Joseph Narrative	83
Joseph's Dreams	85
Be a Blessing	86
Forgiver	86
The Separated One	87
The Threefold Eschatological Aspect	87
Appropriated Eschatology	88
Consummated Eschatology	88
The Threefold Messiah	88
Inter-textual Considerations	89

4. SUMMARY AND CONCLUSION	92
Appendix 1: CHRISTOLOGICAL CONSIDERATIONS OF JOSEPH BY THE EARLY CHURCH FATHERS	94
Appendix 2: KINGDOM PROPHECIES AND ESCHATOLOGY	98
BIBLIOGRAPHY	108
Index of References	122
Index of Authors	129
Subject Index	132

List of Illustrations

1.	The chiastic structure of Genesis 49	53
2.	Interrelations of the Joseph story with Jacob and his family	55
3.	The literary pattern in the Pentateuch	56
4.	The Narrative-Poetry-Epilogue pattern on the micro-structural level	57
5.	The Narrative-Poetry-Epilogue pattern in the Joseph narrative	57
6.	The four major macro-structural patterns in the Pentateuch	60
7.	The structural pattern of the Pentateuch	60
8.	Floorplan of the Tabernacle	63
9.	Map of Canaan and the territories of the twelve tribes of Israel according to the Book of Joshua	71
10.	The genealogies of Messiah ben Joseph, Messiah ben Levi, and Messiah ben David	73
11.	The Joseph narrative	84
12.	The Joseph oracle	84
13.	An outline of Jesus' life	85

List of Tables

1.	Structural overview of the *Testament of the Twelve Patriarchs*	12
2.	Levi and Judah in the *Testament of the Twelve Patriarchs*	13
3.	Joseph in the *Testament of the Twelve Patriarchs*	14
4.	Parallel between T. Benj 3-4:1 and Gen 49:22-26	15
5.	Midreshei Aggadah according to types and periods	28
6.	The apocalyptic midrashim summarized	32
7.	The oracles in Genesis 49	52
8.	The *tōlĕdôt* of Genesis	54
9.	Three major parts of the Joseph oracle	64
10.	Chronology of the Judges	72
11.	Comparison between the Joseph and Judah oracles	74
12.	The age of the Patriarchs	77
13.	Basic elements of biblical typology – Richard M. Davidson	81
14.	Joseph as a type	82
15.	The typological aspects in the Joseph oracle	83

Lists of Abbreviations

Primary Sources: Ancient Texts

Bible Texts and Translations

ET	English Text
LXX	Septuagint
MT	Masoretic Text
Tg.	Targum
Tg. Ps.-J.	Targum Pseudo-Jonathan
t. Tg.	Tosefta Targum

Hebrew Bible/Old Testament

Gen	Genesis	Ezek	Ezekiel
Exod	Exodus	Obad	Obadiah
Lev	Leviticus	Zech	Zechariah
Num	Numbers	Mal	Malachi
Deut	Deuteronomy	Ps/Pss	Psalms
Josh	Joshua	Prov	Proverbs
Judg	Judges	Song	Song of Songs
1-2 Sam	1-2 Samuel	Lam	Lamentations
1-2 Kgs	1-2 Kings	Eccl	Ecclesiastes
Isa	Isiah	Dan	Daniel
Jer	Jeremiah	1-2 Chron	1-2 Chronicles

New Testament

Matt	Matthew	Heb	Hebrews
Rom	Romans	1 Pet	1 Peter
Gal	Galatians	Rev	Revelation
Eph	Ephesians		
Phil	Philippians		

Apocrypha/Pseudepigrapha

1-2 Macc	1-2 Maccabees
4 Macc.	4 Maccabees
1 En.	1 Enoch
3 En.	3 Enoch
Jos. Asen.	Joseph and Aseneth
Sib. Or.	Sibylline Oracles
T. Benj.	Testament of Benjamin
T. Jos	Testament of Joseph
T. Mos.	Testament of Moses
T. Naph.	Testament of Naphtali

Dead Sea Scrolls

Number	Abbreviation	Name
4Q175	4QTest	Testimonia
4Q521	4QMessAp	Messianic Apocalypse
11Q13	11QMelech	Melchizedek

Rabbinic Works

b.	Babylonian Talmud
m.	Mishnah
t.	Tosefta

'Ag. Ber.	'Aggadat Berešit
'Ag. Mash.	'Aggadat Mashiah
Midr.	Midrash
Midr. Tanḥ	Midrash Tanḥuma
Otot	Otot haMasiah
Pesiq. Rab.	Pesiqta Rabbati
Pesiq. Rab Kah	Pesiqta de Rab Kahana
Pirqe R. El.	Pirqe Rabbi Eliezer
Gen. Rab.	Genesis Rabbah
Num. Rab.	Number Rabbah
Song Rab.	Song of Songs Rabbah
Sep. Zerub.	Sefer Zerubbabel
Yal. Shim	Yalquṭ Shimoni

Greek and Latin Works

Ambrose of Milan
Apol. Dav.	*Apologia prophetae David* by Ambrose
Ep.	*Epistolae*
Exh. virginit.	*Exhortatio virginitatis*
Exp. Luc.	*Expositio Evangelii secundum Lucam*
Exp. Ps. 118	*Expositio Psalmi CXVIII*
Jos.	*De Joseph patriarcha*
Off.	*De officiis ministrorum*

Augustine
Civ.	*De civitate Dei (The City of God)*
Enarrat. Ps.	*Enarrationes in Psalmos (Enarrations on the Psalms)*
Gen. litt.	*De Genesi ad litteram (On Genesis Literally Interpreted)*
Quaest. Hept.	*Questions in Heptateuchum*
Serm.	Sermones

Basil of Caesarea
Ep.	*Epistolae*

Bede the Venerable
Gen.	*On Genesis*

Cyprian
Pat.	*De bono patientiae*
Test.	*Ad Quirinum testimonia adversus Judaeos*
Zel. liv.	*De Zelo et livore*

Gregory the Great
Ep.	*Epistolae*
Moral.	*Expositio in Librum Job, sive Moralium libri xxv (Moralia)*

Hippolytus of Rome
Ben. Is. Jac.	*De benedictionibus Isaaci et Jacobi*

Irenaeus
Iren Fragm.	Irenaeus Fragments

Jerome
Comm. Eph.	*Commentariorum in Epistulam ad Ephesios libri III*
Ep. Rip.	*Epistulae ad Riparium presbyterum*

Juvencus
Gen.   *Genesim*

John Chrysostom
Hom. Gen.   *Homiliae in Genesim*
Hom. 1 Thess. *Homiliae in epistulam i ad Thessalonicenses*
Hom. 2 Thess. *Homiliae in epistulam ii ad Thessalonicenses*

Justin Martyr
Dial.   *Dialogus cum Tryphone*

Origen
Cels.   *Contra Celsum*
Hom. Gen.   *Homiliae in Genesim*
Comm. Ser. Matt. Commentarium series in evangelium Matthaei

Schol. Matt. *Scholia in Matthaeum*

Prosper of Aquitaine
Exp. Ps.   *Expositio Psalmorum*

Pseudo-Augustine
Serm.   *Sermones*

Pseudo-Clement
Ep. virg.   *Epistle ad Virgines*

Tertullian
Adv. Jud.   *Adversus Judaeos (Against the Jews)*
Marc.   *Adversus Marcionem*

Zeno of Verona
Tract.   *Tractactus*

Secondary Sources

AB	Anchor Bible
ABD	*Anchor Bible Dictionary*. Edited by David Noel Freedman. 6 vols. New York: Doubleday, 1992.
ACCSOT	Ancient Christian Commentary on Scripture: Old Testament.
ACQ	*American Congregational Quarterly*
AS	*Aramaic Studies*
AUSDDS	*Andrews University Seminary Doctoral Dissertation Series*
AUSS	*Andrews University Seminary Studies*
BA	*Biblical Archaeologist*
BapRev	*Baptist Review*
BDB	Brown, Francis, S. R. Driver, and Charles A. Briggs. *A Hebrew and English Lexicon of the Old Testament*
Bib	*Biblica*
BibInt	Biblical Interpretation Series
BN	*Biblische Notizen*
BR	*Biblical Research*
BRev	*Bible Review*
BSac	*Bibliotheca Sacra*
BYU Studies	*Brigham Young University Studies*
BZ	*Biblische Zeitschrift*
CBQ	*Catholic Biblical Quarterly*
CC	Continental Commentary
CCL	Classic Commentary Library
COT	Commentary on the Old Testament
DARCOM	Daniel and Revelation Committee Series
DNTB	*Dictionary of New Testament Background*. Edited by Craig A. Evans and Stanley E. Porter. Downers Grove, IL: InterVarsity Press, 2000.

EDSS	*Encyclopedia of the Dead Sea Scrolls.* Edited by Lawrence H. Schiffman and James C. VanderKam. 2 vols. New York: Oxford University Press, 2000.
EncJud	*Encyclopedia Judaica.* Edited by Fred Skolnik and Michael Berenbaum. 2nd ed. 22 vols. Detroit: Macmillian Reference USA, 2007.
EVQ	*Evangelical Quarterly*
ExpTim	*Expository Times*
HTR	*Harvard Theological Review*
HTS	*Harvard Theological Studies*
HUCA	*Hebrew Union College Annual*
IDB	*The Interpreter's Dictionary of the Bible.* Edited by George A. Buttrick. 4 vols. New York: Abingdon, 1962.
Int	*Interpretation*
ISBE	*International Standard Bible Encyclopedia.* Edited by Geoffrey W. Bromiley. 4 vols. Grand Rapids: Eerdmans, 1979-1988
JAAR	*Journal of the American Academy of Religion*
JATS	*Journal of the Adventist Theological Society*
JBL	*Journal of Biblical Literature*
JBQ	*Jewish Bible Quarterly*
JETS	*Journal of the Evangelical Theological Society*
JNES	*Journal of Near Eastern Studies*
JSBLE	*Journal of the Society of Biblical Literature and Exegesis*
JSNT	*Journal for the Study of the New Testament*
JSOT	*Journal for the Study of the Old Testament*
JSOTSup	Journal for the Study of the Old Testament Supplement Series
JSP	*Journal for the Study of the Pseudepigrapha*
JSPSup	Journal for the Study of the Pseudepigrapha Supplement Series
JTS	*Journal of Theological Studies*
NEASB	*Near East Archaelogical Society Bulletin*
NICOT	New International Commentary of the Old Testament

NIDOTTE	*New International Dictionary of Old Testament Theology and Exegesis*. Edited by Willem A. VanGemeren. 5 vols. Grand Rapids: Zondervan, 1997.
NovT	*Novum Testamentum*
NTS	*New Testament Studies*
OTL	Old Testament Library
PCSBR	*Papers of the Chicago Society of Biblical Research*
PSBA	*Proceedings of the Society of Biblical Archaeology*
RevQ	*Revue de Qumran*
RRJ	*Review of Rabbinic Judaism*
SBJT	*Southern Baptist Journal of Theology*
ScEs	*Science et esprit*
SCS	Septuagint and Cognate Studies
SDABC	*Seventh-day Adventist Biblical Commentary*
SNTSMS	Society for New Testament Studies Monograph Series
STRev	*Sewanee Theological Review*
SVTP	Studia in Veteris Testamenti Pseudepigraphica
TJ	*Trinity Journal*
TOTC	Tyndale Old Testament Commentary
TWOT	*Theological Wordbook of the Old Testament*. Edited by R. Laird Harris, Gleason L. Archer Jr., and Bruce K. Waltke. 2 vols. Chicago: Moody Press, 1980.
VT	*Vetus Testamentum*
WBC	Word Biblical Commentary
WC	Westminster Commentaries
YJL	Yale Judaica Series
ZAW	*Zeitschrift für die alttestamentliche Wissenschaft*
ZNW	*Zeitschrift für die neutestamentliche Wissenschaft und die Kunde der älteren Kirche*

Introduction

In Genesis 49, Jacob reveals, through his blessings, what will happen to his sons and their descendants in the days to come. At this time Joseph was the vizier, the elder statesman, and the Chief Steward of Egypt. Jacob and his clan had been given desirable agricultural land in Egypt, but God's promise to Abraham was in jeopardy. Although Jacob's offspring were increasing and they were, seemingly, a blessing to the people, they had not settled down in the promised land. Thus, Jacob's Genesis 49 blessing was very important. It expressed what would happen in the future with the Abrahamic covenant and it also revealed who would be the new heir after Jacob's death.

While Genesis 49 focuses equally on Judah and Joseph, Jacob has only brief and general blessings for his other ten sons. Judah has often been considered Jacob's successor and the true heir based on Jacob's words in Gen 49:8-12. Indeed, these verses reveal Judah's leadership and kingship, and they also state that Shiloh, Messiah, will come from his descendants. So much focus has been placed on the Judah blessing that the Joseph blessing has fallen completely into the background and, in many cases, just ignored. However, some contradictions become apparent when carefully considering the Joseph blessing which suggest Joseph was the successor of Jacob, a ruler among his brothers, and even hints that the Messiah will be his descendant. This being the case, how should the Joseph blessing be understood and does it really have a messianic aspect? If it has a messianic aspect, should the blessing be considered as a messianic prophecy or is Joseph merely a messianic type? Also, what is the nature of the relationship between the blessings conferred upon Judah and those conferred upon Joseph?

This study will analyze Gen 49:22-26 to determine if there is a messianic/eschatological significance in the Joseph blessing as it was expressed by Jacob. If there is, this study will also attempt to identify the extent of this significance. It is hoped this study will shed some light on the topic of the potential messianic aspect of the Joseph blessing and contribute to the growing body of research regarding this topic.

Within the Jewish tradition there is an expectation of a Messiah ben Joseph who will have an important function in the eschatological age. Within the Christian tradition, scholars often suggest Joseph is a type of the New Testament Messiah but do so without providing a strong scriptural foundation for this typological reading of the Joseph narrative. It is problematic to point only to similarities between Joseph's and Jesus' lives and conclude that the one must be foreshadowing the other, as these resemblances could just be mere coincidence. Given this, this study will attempt to do two things. Firstly, it will endeavor to determine whether the final redactor of the Joseph narrative intended Joseph to be a type of the future Messiah – a finding that would be relevant for both Jewish and Christian faith traditions. Secondly, within the Jewish context, if Joseph is indeed a type of the suffering Messiah, then Joseph could fill the developmental gap between the messianic promise in Gen 3:15 and the suffering servant theme in the prophetic writings—providing a fertile base for the Messiah ben Joseph belief in later rabbinic traditions. Within the Christian context, this study will attempt to build a scriptural basis for considering whether Joseph is a type of Christ. Among evangelical scholars there are four different views of typology as outlined by W. Edward Glenny. These are the covenant view, the revised dispensational view, the progressive dispensational view, and the view of Richard M. Davidson.[1] This study will consider the Joseph narrative in light of Davidson's view of typology[2] to identify "if the scriptures do clearly indicate the predictive quality of these OT types before their fulfillment"—a criticism voiced by Glenny.[3] Thus, this study will also function as a test case of Davidson's methodology.

In this publication, Chapter 1 presents the history of interpretation of Gensis 49. It examines both the Jewish and Christian documents that deal with this passage and with Joseph in general. The Jewish belief in the Messiah, son of Joseph, and the early Christian teaching that Joseph foreshadowed Jesus' life and mission is explored. It should be noted that the history of interpretation focuses on the Second Temple period and later Rabbinic writings and deals only briefly with the early and present Christian views. This study

---

[1] W. Edward Glenny, "Typology: A Summary of the Present Evangelical Discussion," *JETS* 40 (1997): 627-38.

[2] Richard M. Davidson, *Typology in Scripture: A Study of Hermeneutical τύπος Structures*, AUSDDS 2 (Berrien Springs, MI: Andrews University Press, 1981).

[3] Glenny, "Typology," 637.

is limited to the Joseph oracle in Gen 49. However, when relevant, it refers to the other messianic passages both in the Pentateuch and in the rest of the Hebrew scripture. Further research is certainly warranted and needed, given the sheer scope of this topic. Chapter 2 provides a possible translation and gives literary notes regarding the Joseph oracle. It also offers a contextual analysis which deals with the immediate context of the oracle, the outline of the Joseph narrative, and the purpose and outline of the Pentateuch. Chapter 3 considers the messianic and eschatological implications of the Joseph oracle. Firstly, it identifies the messianic aspects found in Jacob's vision about Joseph, and examines the relationship between the Judah and Joseph oracles. It then shows the eschatological aspects which are the fulfillment of the prophecy. Lastly, the chapter demonstrates how the findings of this study relate to other messianic passages in the Pentateuch. Chapter 4 provides a brief the summary and conclusion of the findings.

1. HISTORY OF INTERPRETATION

Traditionally, it was widely believed the poetic words recorded in Gen 49 and Deut 33 were spoken by Jacob to his sons and by Moses to the tribes of Israel, respectively. However, with the rise of critical scholarship, Joel Heck notes this is no longer the consensus view. Today, the predominant interpretation is held by critical scholars who argue that these two chapters contain individual "blessings," composed by different authors at different times, which were later selected and put down in writing. It is believed these "blessings" are pre-monarchic and could be dated to the period of the Judges, although parts of the blessing regarding Judah could be later.[1] Following this stream of interpretation, there is no literary unity in these two chapters nor were these chapters a part of an "original" Pentateuchal narrative. Accordingly, these "blessings" may just be a result of a religious and political agenda or movement in Israel.

This chapter limits the history of interpretation to Gen 49, with an emphasis on the Joseph oracle (Gen 49:22-26). Although Deut 33 is not the focus of this chapter, it is referred to because of its strong parallels to Gen 49. In this attempt, however, it is necessary to examine both Jewish and Christian literature which provide insights regarding the story of Joseph because this may shed some light on how the Joseph oracle and narrative have been perceived throughout history. The Jewish belief in a Messiah from the house of Joseph[2] and the early Christian teaching that Joseph was a type for Jesus

---

[1] Joel D. Heck, "A History of Interpretation of Genesis 49 and Deuteronomy 33," *BSac* 147 (1990): 16-18; see also, Frank Moore Cross, Jr. and David Noel Freedman, *Studies in Ancient Yahwistic Poetry* (Grand Rapids: Eerdmans, 1975), 46-47.

[2] There are other names and genealogies given for Messiah ben Joseph in Jewish literature. R. Machir and Saadia Gaon called him *Nehemia ben Husiel*, and R. Elieser gave him the name *Menachem ben Ammiel*. For further study see J. F. Morton, "The Doctrine of the Two Messiahs Among the Jews," *BapRev* 9 (1881): 67. In the Targumim he was named *Messiah bar/ben Ephraim* (t. Tg. Zech 12:10; Tg. Ps.-J. on Exod 40.9-11; Tg. Song 4.5; 7.4), and *Ephraim Messiah* (Pesiq. Rab. 34.36-37; Midr. Aleph Beth 11b.15) or *War Messiah* (Gen. Rab. 75.6; 99.2; Midr. Tanḥ. 11.3

are of special interest.³ The history of interpretation will consider relevant passages in Second Temple period literature, the Messiah ben Joseph tradition in Rabbinic Judaism, and the type-antitype, Joseph-Jesus interpretation in early Christian texts—a brief discussion on the development seen in later Christian texts is also provided.⁴

At this point, a few complicating factors need to be mentioned. The first is the format of the Second Temple period writings. These writings comment on some of the problematic verses from the Hebrew scripture, but they do not present the comments in the same form as most of today's commentaries which have exegesis verse for verse. Instead, these writings present the theological points in story form, often using certain keywords which would allude to the biblical passage being examined. The second problem is the dating of some of the remarks in the earlier Jewish writings. Since some of this literature was written over an extended period of time, one cannot be certain when specific statements were written. Third, it is difficult to establish the religious background of some of the literature from the late Second Temple period. It could be Jewish, Christian, originally Jewish but later edited when non-Jewish Christians assumed these writings, or even the work of a

---

[I.103a]; Pesiq. Rab. 8.4; 15.14/15; Pesiq. Rab Kah. 5.9; Song Rab. 2.13.4; Num. Rab. 14.1) in midrashic literature. In the Dead Sea Scrolls, he may be identified with the Josephite Messiah (4Q175 [4QTest]), see David C. Mitchell, "Rabbi Dosa and the Rabbis Differ: Messiah ben Joseph in the Babylonian Talmud," *RBJ* 8.1 (2005): 89.

³ See the comments by Hippolytus (170–235 CE), Ephrem the Syrian (306–373 CE), Ambrose of Milan (340–397 CE), and Rufinus of Aquileia (340–410 CE) collected in Mark Sheridan, *Genesis 12-50*, ACCSOT 2 (Downers Grove, IL: InterVarsity Press, 2002), 343-47. Nicholas P. Lunn argues the allusions appearing in the Synoptic Gospels and Acts to the Joseph narrative supports the notion that Joseph was viewed as a biblical type of Jesus by Luke and the first Christians and became a part of the Christian exegetical tradition (see, "Allusions to the Joseph Narrative in the Synoptic Gospels and Acts: Foundations of a Biblical Type," *JETS* 55.1 [2012]: 27-41). See also Kristian S. Heal, "Joseph as a Type of Christ in Syriac Literature," *BYU Studies* 41.1 (2002): 29-49.

⁴ This history of interpretation will not look at the Samaritan tradition about the Messiah ben Joseph since most scholars agree that the Jewish and the Samaritan tradition developed individually. It is not logical that Jews would borrow a set of beliefs from the Samaritans or vice versa, due to their hostile relationship. However, it would be reasonable to assume that both traditions developed from the Scripture.

Christian convert from Judaism. Fourth, some of the original sources are difficult to determine, which makes it necessary to quote a secondary source.

Inner-Biblical Interpretation

The logical place to start the history of interpretation is by looking at the Hebrew scripture itself. It is interesting to note the prominent role the Joseph narrative has in the book of Genesis. Its prominence is rivaled only by the narratives of Abraham and Jacob. In spite of this central position, Joseph receives only scant attention in the rest of the TaNaKh. The remainder of the Pentateuch, for instance, refers to the person Joseph only two more times. The first is found in Exod 1:8 (referring indirectly to his service in Egypt), and the second in Exod 13:19, which is the fulfillment of Israel's oath to Joseph (Gen 50:25). The book of Joshua concludes by stating Joseph's bones were buried in Shechem (Josh 24:32). Joseph had, in a sense, been with the Israelites through their whole sojourn in Egypt, the Exodus experience, and the conquest of the promised land. It could be argued that Joseph's bones are proverbial bookends of the Exodus/Conquest story. It is the last thing mentioned in the book of Genesis, setting the stage for the Exodus, and is the closing note on which the book of Joshua rests and the Exodus/Conquest story concludes. First Chronicles 5:1-2 states that Joseph received the right of the firstborn. Two passages in the book of Psalms refer to Joseph or could be understood as a reference to the people of Israel: (1) Psalm 81:5-6 may refer to Joseph's experience in Egypt, and (2) Psalm 105:16-22 refers to the Joseph narrative, with an emphasis on Joseph's statements in Gen 45:5-8 and 50:20.[5]

> All other references to "Joseph" are either to the twin tribes Ephraim and Manasseh (Gen. 49:22, 26; Deut. 27:12; 33:13; Ezek. 47:13; 48:32; et al.), or to the Northern Israelite Kingdom in general (Ezek. 37:16, 19; Amos 5:15; 6:6; Ps. 78:67), otherwise referred to as the "House of Joseph" (Amos 5:6; Obad. 18; Zech. 10:6; cf. Judg. 1:22, 23, 35; II Sam. 19:21; I King 11:28).[6]

---

[5] Nahum M. Sarna, "Joseph," *EncJud* 11:409.
[6] Ibid., 409-10.

Nothing overtly negative is ever mentioned about Joseph in the TaNaKh. Daniel is the only other main character who readily comes to mind in the Hebrew Scripture as one who is also portrayed in such a positive light. When comparing these two men's lives, some fascinating parallels become evident. They were about the same age when they were taken away from their home. Both were dreamers and interpreters of dreams. Both ended up second in command in their kingdom of exile. Their faith in God was tested to the extreme. When reading the Hebrew Scripture, it becomes clear that Joseph was regarded as a very real person who was considered an extraordinary man by the Israelites.

Early Jewish Interpretation (Scribal Exegesis before 70 CE)
Septuagint

The Septuagint is probably the earliest Jewish interpretation of the Hebrew Bible. It dates to the third century BCE and was the first translation of the Scripture into another language. It was translated into Greek for the Jewish diaspora in Alexandria who had been forced by circumstance to abandon their language.[7] This version has had a great impact on both Jewish and Christian literature, and was probably the primary Old Testament source for the writers of the New Testament. The Septuagint was also the version used by the Early Church Fathers. It is noteworthy that the Septuagint (LXX) is an older version than the Masoretic Text (MT), which dates from the period 500–1000 CE. In spite of this, most scholars agree that, after the Dead Sea Scrolls were discovered, the MT was more accurate to the "original" text than the LXX.

A translation is always an interpretation, regardless of how accurately a translator tries to follow the original text. The scope of a word in one language might be very different than in another. Another translation issue pertains to how a text should be translated, whether literal, idiomatic, paraphrasic, or midrashic. It is also a possibility that the translator has misunderstood or tried to smooth out some of the difficulties within the text.[8] While this study does not look at every text in the Septuagint that relates to Joseph, it does refer to the LXX when it differs significantly from the MT. This is especially important in chapter 2, which translates and comments on the Joseph oracle.

---

[7] Sven K. Soderlund, "Septuagint," *ISBE* 4:400.
[8] Ibid., 401.

Extra-Canonical Writings

The first unambiguous mention of Messiah ben Joseph/Ephraim appears in the tannaitic period, in passages difficult to date (b. Sukkah 52a; Tg. Ps.-J. Exod 40:11; Tg. Song 4:5; t. Tg. Zech 12:10).[9] Thus, the predominant view held by scholars is that the idea of Messiah ben Joseph developed and was later written down in the Talmud after the destruction of the temple (70 CE), the failure of the Bar Kokhba revolt (132–35 CE),[10] and the Hadrianic persecution (132–36 CE). Their reasoning suggests this is the historical event that would create a need for the doctrine of a suffering and militant Messiah. Martha Himmelfarb makes a different case and argues the weight of the evidence suggest "the figure of the messiah son of Joseph developed as a popular Jewish response to the Christian narrative, an attempt to provide Jews with a dying and rising savior of their own."[11] Jacques Doukhan makes a similar case based on the sparse reference to Messiah ben Joseph in early Jewish literature: "This [b. Sukkah 52a] is the only passage in all the Talmud which speaks of two Messiahs. It is possible therefore to think that we have here a late addition contemporaneous with the Midrashim and with the Jewish apocalypses, which reflect the Jewish-Christian polemics."[12] In contrast, David C. Mitchell argues Messiah ben Joseph is not a rabbinic invention, rather he makes the case this belief predates Christianity and could be traced to the earliest part of the Hebrew Scriptures which was also the traditional rabbinic view prior to the Renaissance. He writes: "My own position is that Messiah ben Joseph is implicit in all essentials in the Pentateuch. And more, that from early times, his death was seen as sacrificial and atoning."[13]

---

[9] Gerald J. Blidstein, "Messiah in Rabbinic Thought," *EncJud* 14:112.

[10] Joseph Heineman, "The Messiah of Ephraim and the Premature Exodus of the Tribe of Ephraim," in *Messianism in the Talmudic Era*, ed. Leo Landman (New York: Ktav, 1979), 340-41.

[11] Martha Himmelfarb, "The Messiah Son of Joseph in Ancient Judaism," in *Envisioning Judaism: Studies in Honor of Peter Schäfer on the Occasion of his Seventieth Birthday*, ed. Ra'anan S. Boustan et al. (Tübingen: Mohr Siebeck, 2013), 2:790.

[12] Jacques B. Doukhan, *Drinking at the Sources: An Appeal to the Jew and the Christian to Note Their Common Beginnings*, trans. Walter R. Beach and Robert M. Johnston (Mountain View, CA: Pacific Press, 1981), 130, n.116.

[13] David C. Mitchell, *Messiah ben Joseph* (Newton Mearns, Scotland: Campbell Publications, 2016), 9.

Pseudepigraphic Writings

The Pseudepigraphic writings[14] often comment on the Hebrew scripture[15] and provide the reader with an invaluable insight into the intellectual, social, and spiritual history of late Second Temple period Judaism.[16] Charlesworth observes: "It is now widely recognized that the Jewish pseudepigrapha that antedate c. 135 CE represent a chapter in early Jewish exegesis. The early Jewish writings collected in the Pseudepigrapha are chronologically much closer to the commencement of Jewish exegesis than post–70 Jewish works." He adds, "biblical exegesis is the crucible of the Pseudepigrapha. In it ancient humanity's wisdom, scientific observation, and speculations were melted down and shaped to reappear as Jewish tradition."[17] The Pseudepigrapha is not only important for the study of Early Judaism but it also provides an essential background context for New Testament studies. Charles Fritsch states: "No one can understand the religious development of later Judaism or the background of the New Testament without studying the Jewish outside books. They serve as a bridge between the Old Testament and New Testament, supplementing much that is found in the Hebrew scriptures, and heralding new ideas which appear in the New Testament records."[18]

This study takes a closer look at three literary works which have special relevance to the history of interpretation—the *Testament of the Twelve Patriarchs*, *Joseph and Asenath*, and *3 Enoch*.

---

[14] The Pseudepigrapha is a collection of writings dating from the period between c. 300 BCE and 200 CE. These documents were written by Jews and possibly Christian-Jews and/or Christians in honor of and inspired by Old Testament heroes (see James H. Charlesworth and P. Dykers, *Pseudepigrapha and Modern Research*, SCS 7 [Missoula, MT: Scholars Press for the Society of Biblical Literature, 1976], 25).

[15] See James H. Charlesworth and Craig A. Evans, eds., *The Pseudepigrapha and Early Biblical Interpretation*, JSPSup 14 (Sheffield: JSOT Press, 1993).

[16] James A. Sanders, "Introduction: Why the Pseudepigrapha?" in *The Pseudepigrapha and Early Biblical Interpretation*, ed. James H. Charlesworth and Craig A. Evans; JSPSup 14 (Sheffield: JSOT Press, 1993), 14.

[17] James H. Charlesworth, "In the Crucible: The Pseudepigrapha as Biblical Interpreation," in *The Pseudepigrapha and Early Biblical Interpretation*, ed. James H. Charlesworth and Craig A. Evans (Sheffield: JSOT Press, 1993), 22.

[18] Charles T. Fritsch, "Pseudepigrapha," *IDB* 3:963.

Testament of the Twelve Patriarchs

The *Testament of the Twelve Patriarchs* was probably written by a Hellenized Jew sometime in the early second century BCE[19] and redacted in the second century CE by a Christian.[20] The date and origin of this document have been widely debated, with the two most prominent scholars in this controversy being James H. Charlesworth and M. de Jonge. Charlesworth argues for an early Jewish origin, while de Jonge argues for a second-century Christian origin.[21] This study holds Charlesworth's position because fragments of the T. Levi, T. Naph., and T. Juda have been found among the Dead Sea Scrolls, supporting Jewish authorship.

The *Testament of the Twelve Patriarchs* is a Jewish document based on the Joseph narrative and emphasizes Jacob's last words to his twelve sons as recorded in Gen 49. The deathbed scene in the first two verses of the chapter is the framework for each of the testaments.

Genesis 49:1-2

¹Then Jacob called for his sons and said: "Gather around so that I can tell you what will happen to you in days to come. ²Assemble and listen, sons of Jacob; listen to your father Israel" (NAS)

¹ וַיִּקְרָא יַעֲקֹב אֶל־בָּנָיו וַיֹּאמֶר הֵאָסְפוּ וְאַגִּידָה לָכֶם אֵת אֲשֶׁר־יִקְרָא אֶתְכֶם בְּאַחֲרִית הַיָּמִים:
² הִקָּבְצוּ וְשִׁמְעוּ בְּנֵי יַעֲקֹב וְשִׁמְעוּ אֶל־יִשְׂרָאֵל אֲבִיכֶם:

---

[19] H. C. Kee, "Testament of the Twelve Patriarchs: A New Translation and Introduction," in *The Old Testament Pseudepigrapha*, ed. James Charlesworth (New York: Doubleday, 1983), 1:777-78.

[20] Charlesworth, "In the Crucible: The Pseudepigrapha as Biblical Interpretation," 33.

[21] See: Harm W. Hollander and Marinus de Jonge, *The Testament of the Twelve Patriarchs: A Commentary*, SVTP 8 (Leiden: Brill, 1985), and James H. Charlesworth, *The Old Testament Pseudepigrapha and the New Testament: Prolegomena for the Study of Christian Origins*, SNTSMS 54 (New York: Cambridge University Press, 1985), and Marinus de Jonge, ed., *The Testament of the Twelve Patriarchs: Text and Interpretation*, SVTP 3 (Leiden: Brill, 1975), and Marinus de Jonge, *The Testament of the Twelve Patriarchs: A Study of Their Text, Composition and Origin* (Assen: Van Gorcum, 1953).

As Jacob blessed each of his sons before he died, so did his sons bless their children when they were about to die. The difference between the two accounts is the apocalyptic emphasis. While Gen 49:1 states, אֶת־אֲשֶׁר־יִקְרָא אֶתְכֶם בְּאַחֲרִית הַיָּמִים, *that I can tell you what will happen to you in days to come,*" the *Testament of the Twelve Patriarchs* fills in this statement with lengthy apocalyptic additions, see Table 1.[22] Howard C. Kee notes that each of the twelve testaments contains six key elements. These elements have been utilized when creating Table 1 and are: 1) introduction to the testament, the setting; 2) narrative of the life of the patriarch; 3) ethical exhortation; 4) prediction regarding the future, an apocalyptic section; followed by 5) a second exhortation; and is concluded by 6) the death and burial of said patriarch.

Two messianic figures emerge in this document: the priestly and the royal Messiahs. J. Liver created a table (see Table 2) which shows the attitude toward Levi and Judah in the different Testaments. Table 3 shows the passages in the document which relate to Joseph.

Many scholars focus on the dual Messiah in this document, while ignoring the role of Joseph. Haram W. Hollander contends that Joseph is an ethical model in the *Testament of the Twelve Patriarchs*. He writes:

> In T. Benj., the twelfth and last testament of the Testaments, the author has summed up all the scattered statements concerning his ethical ideal of man in one continuous discourse. This resume centers around the 'good man', the personification of this ideal. And since Joseph is the good man per excellence, it is he who is introduced as an illuminating example.[23]

---

[22] Charlesworth, "In the Crucible," 32-34.

[23] Harm W. Hollander, *Joseph as an Ethical Model in the Testaments of the Twelve Patriarchs*, ed. A. M. Denis and M. de Jonge, SVTP 6 (Leiden: Brill, 1981), 91.

Table 1. Structural overview of the *Testament of the Twelve Patriarchs*

SON	Intro.	Narrative of their Life	Ethical Exhortation	Prediction Regarding Future	Second Exhortation	Death and Burial
Ruben	1:1-5	1:6-3:15	4:1-6:4	6:5-7	6:8-12	7:1-2
Simeon	1:1-2	2:1-13	3:1-5:3	5:4-6:7 (6:5, 7)	7:1-3	7:4-9:2
Levi	1:1-2	2:1-12:5 (2:11; 4:1, 4; 10:2-3)	13:1-9	14:1-18:14 (14:1, 2; 16:3; 17:2; 18:7, 9)	19:1-4a	19:4b-5
Judah	1:1-6	2:1-12:12	13:1-20:5	21:1-25:5 (24:4)	26:1	26:2-4
Issachar	1:1	1:2-3:8	4:1-5:8	6:1-4	7:1-7 (7:7)	7:8-9
Zebulon	1:1-2	1:3-4:13	5:1-8:1	8:2-10:4 (9:8)	10:5	10:6
Dan	1:1-2	1:3-9	2:1-5:5	5:6-13 (5:10, 13)	6:1-11 (6:7, 9)	7:1-3
Naphtali	1:1-4	1:5-2:8	2:9-3:5	4:1-8:1	8:2-10 (8:2, 3)	9:1-2
Gad	1:1-2	1:3-2:5	3:1-7:7	8:1-2 (8:2)	8:3a	8:3b-4
Asher	1:1-2	–	1:3-6:5	7:1-3 (7:3)	7:4-7	8:1-2
Joseph	1:1	1:2-16:5	17:1-18:4	19:1-10 (19:8)	19:11-12 (19:11)	20:1-6
Benjamin	1:1-6	2:1-5	3:1-8:3 (3:8)	9:1-3 (9:3-5)	10:1-11:5 (10:7, 8, 9)	12:1-4

Source: Jan A. Sigvartsen, "The Afterlife Views and the Use of the Tanakh in Support of the Resurrection Concept in the Literature of Second Temple Period Judaism: The Apocrypha and the Pseudepigrapha" (PhD diss., Andrews University, 2006), 218.

Table 2. Levi and Judah in the *Testament of the Twelve Patriarchs*

Themes	Reu.	Sim.	Levi	Jud.	Iss.	Dan	Naph.	Gad	Jos.
Superiority of Levi over Judah	6:7,11			21:1-2 25:1-2			5:3-4		
Priesthood to Levi; Kingship to Judah	6:8,10	7:2	8:11-16			5:7			
Salvation of Israel in Levi and Judah		7:1				5:4,7	8:2-3	8:1	19:11
The new priest at the end of days	6:8	7:2?	18:1*ff.*	24:1-4?					
The messianic King at the end of days	6:12	7:2?		22:2-3 24:5-6					

Source: J. Liver, "The Doctrine of the Two Messiahs in Sectarian Literature in the Time of the Second Commonwealth," *HTR* 52.3 (1959): 178.

Table 3. Joseph in the *Testament of the Twelve Patriarchs*

Themes	Reu.	Sim.	Zeb.	Dan	Naph.	Gad	Jos.	Benj.
Joseph as an example of perfection or morality	4:8-11	4:4-9	2:3 8:4	1:4			3-17	3:1*ff.*
Joseph portrayed in a negative light						5:7		
Joseph's bones a blessing		8:3					20:2	
Joseph's rulership or superiority	6:7				5:7 6:6		1:1 18:4 19:12	4:1
Joseph, the savior of the world, and God's lamb								3:8

The passage found in the *Testament of Benjamin* 3:8 is probably the most important passage for this study in which Jacob states:

Greek (c and β) textual tradition

'Through you [Joseph] will be fulfilled the heavenly prophecy concerning the Lamb of God, the Savior of the world, because the unspotted one will be betrayed by lawless men, and the sinless one will die for impious men by the blood of the covenant for the salvation of the gentiles and of Israel and the destruction of Beliar and his servant.'

Armenian textual tradition

'In you [Joseph] will be fulfilled the heavenly prophecy which says that the spotless one will be defiled by lawless men and the sinless one will die for the sake of impious men.'

In this passage, a future descendant of Joseph is portrayed as the Lamb of God who will die to bring salvation to humankind.[24] The close parallel between T. Benj. 3-4:1 and Gen 49:22-26, which is shown in Table 4, lends strong support to one passage being an explanation of the other. Thus, from this parallel one could argue that T. Benj. 3:8 is an interpretation of Gen 49:24c, which states: מִשָּׁם רֹעֶה אֶבֶן יִשְׂרָאֵל, *From there, the shepherd, the stone of Israel.*

Table 4. Parallel between T. Benj. 3:1-4:1 and Gen 49:22-26

Testament of Benjamin 3:1-4:1	Genesis 49:22-26
3:1-2	49:22
3:3	49:23
3:4-5	49:24a-b
3:8	49:24c
4:1	49:26d

There is one other text in the *Testament of the Twelve Patriarchs* which refers to the "the Lamb of God." This text, found in the *Testament of Joseph*, states,

> And I saw that a virgin was born from Judah, wearing a linen stole; and from her was born a spotless lamb.... Honor Levi and Judah, because from their seed will arise the Lamb of God who will take away the sin of the world, and will save all the nations, as well as Israel (T. Jos. 19:8.11).

This citation indicates that the Lamb of God will also arise from the tribes of Levi and Judah. From these two passages one can conclude that the *Testament of the Twelve Patriarchs* implies a person will emerge from Levi, Judah, and Joseph who will be called the Lamb of God, be spotless, and bring salvation to humankind. Is this a Jewish belief or a later Christian interpolation? Did the Jews before Jesus Christ look for the Messiah who would be

---

[24] Although the Armenian version does not mention the aspect of the 'Lamb of God,' it still carries the redemptive aspect.

called the Lamb of God and would "take away the sin of the world," or did a Christian editor or author add references or allusions to the messianic figures to strengthen their believers' faith? If this belief is a product of pre-Christian Judaism, this would indicate beliefs often attributed to Christianity actually have their origin in Judaism as an extension of martyrology seen in Apocrypha and the Pseudepigrapha (e.g. 2 Macc 7; T. Mos. 9:7–10:3; 4 Macc 9–18)[25] and the suffering servant as described in the Dead Sea Scrolls[26]—where a righteous martyr has an atoning function for God's people as a whole. If it is Christian, why did the Christian writer expect three messianic figures when the Christian movement only expected one messiah?[27] If the passage is indeed Jewish, but written in the Christian era, why would the Jewish writer adopt an idea about a suffering Savior from the Christians? Were they trying to compete with a Christian narrative? These are interesting questions indeed, but are beyond the scope of this study which accepts there is sufficient support for pre-Christian Jewish authorship for this passage.

The Lamb of God

Most scholars would argue the passage concerning the Lamb of God has a Christian origin[28] due to its Christian language. They would claim that the idea of the Lamb of God was first introduced by John the Baptist (John 1:29, 36). This argument would make sense if the Lamb of God only referred to Judah, but, as shown above, this phrase was also used for Levi and Joseph.[29] J. C. O'Neill contends:

---

[25] W. J. Heard and C. A. Evans, "Revolutionary Movements, Jewish," *DNTB*, 941-44.

[26] See Israel Knohl, *The Messiah before Jesus: The Suffering Servant of the Dead Sea Scrolls* (Berkeley: University of California Press, 2000).

[27] de Jonge, *Testament of the Twelve Patriarchs*, 9.

[28] See Hollander and de Jonge, *Testament of the Twelve Patriarchs*, 408-9, 419-20; M. de Jonge, "Christian Influence in the Testaments of the Twelve Patriarchs," in *Studies on the Testaments of the Twelve Patriarchs*, ed. M. de Jonge (Leiden: Brill, 1975), 193-246; and Kee, "Testament of the Twelve Patriarchs," 1:824-26.

[29] There is a Jewish tradition (*haggadah*) dating to the 3rd century BCE dealing with a dream Pharaoh had about a lamb that would outweigh the whole land of Egypt. Although this vision refers to Moses and the exodus, it is still important that the concept of a lamb-savior was already a part of Jewish thought long before the Christian era. For further study, see Klaus Koch, "Das Lamm, das Ägypten vernichtet: Ein Fragment aus Jannes und Jambres und sein geschichtlicher Hinter-

> As the text stands, the reference to the lamb is unlikely to be Christian. We should have to imagine a Christian's wanting to insert a reference to Jesus the Lamb of God in a context where another great figure shares in his work. The passage seems to assume a doctrine of the two anointed figures, the anointed priest and the anointed king.... In other words, the lamb has been locked into the tradition by a scribe who held a theory of two Messiahs.[30]

He continues:

> The language is so familiar that we can hardly entertain the possibility that it is not Christian. Christian, however it can hardly be. Although early Christian writers like Melito of Sardis and Justin Martyr recognize in the patriarch Joseph a prototype of Jesus Christ, no Christian writer would ever have called a Messiah ben Joseph Lamb of God, for Jesus was of the tribe of Judah.[31]

It is almost certain that the Jews did expect a Messiah who could be called the "Lamb of God." All aspects in the Lamb of God texts are rooted in the Jewish scripture, and it would be unreasonable to believe the Jews were not aware of them. The early Christians were themselves Jews and had been brought up with Jewish writings and traditions. When they accepted Jesus as their Messiah, they did not leave the Jewish religion. Rather, this new doctrine was merely added to their Jewish faith. It would be reasonable to suggest John the Baptist considered Jesus as the fulfillment of the "Lamb of God" spoken of in Jewish Scripture and tradition, particularly since he belonged to a priestly family.

G. H. Dix suggests, concerning the Joseph blessing in T. Benj. 3:8, there are only two predictions in the Old Testament which can be described as "the heavenly prophecy which says that the blameless one should be de-

---

grund," *ZNW* 57 (1966): 79-93; Christoph Burchard, "Das Lamm in der Waagschale: Herkunft und Hintergrund eines haggadischen Midraschs zu Ex 1:15-22," *ZNW* 57 (1966): 219-28; and Tg. Ps.-J on Exod 1:15; 7:11 and Num 22:22.

[30] J. C. O'Neill, "The Lamb of God in the Testament of the Twelve Patriarchs," *JSNT* 2 (1979): 4.

[31] Ibid., 7.

filed for lawless men, the sinless one shall die for ungodly men."[32] He continues:

> The first of these is the four Songs of the Suffering Servant [Isa 52:13-53:12], and the second Zechariah xii 9 ff.[33] Consequently this Jewish writing associates a descendant of Joseph with one, or both, of these passages.... He [the Suffering Servant] resembles Joseph in that his undeserved sufferings bring salvation; but he is a transcendental Joseph, made to be such by the influence of the Messiah ben Joseph theme, as the testimony of the later Jewish rabbis also bears witness, since they interpreted the prediction as referring to this suffering, dying Messiah of ancient tradition.[34]

It is important, however, to note that the author of the T. Benj. 3:8 does not label this sinless, suffering, and dying Josephite as Messiah ben Joseph. In fact, the Testament uses the title "Messiah" only for Levi and Judah. If the author did not believe this Josephite was the Messiah, why did he make him "sinless"? Dix suggests the following explanation:

> There was a tradition already existing in some circles that the Songs and the Zechariah prophecy indicated an individual, that this individual was to be the Messiah ben Joseph, and that the writer of the Testament modified this tradition slightly: because of his belief in a Messiah ben Levi, he could not accept the hope of a Messiah ben Joseph, but he accepted as much of it as he could, viz. that the Suffering Servant should be a 'sinless' Josephite who should die on Israel's behalf.[35]

---

[32] G. H. Dix, "Notes and Studies: The Messiah Ben Joseph," *JTS* 28 (1925-26): 135.

[33] Although the interpretation of this prophecy has been disputed, it is still of great importance since the first Christians quoted it as a prediction of Jesus' suffering and death, and the Jewish rabbis used it as a prediction of the suffering Messiah ben Joseph.

[34] Dix, "Notes and Studies," 135, 140.

[35] Ibid., 135-36.

In this context, it is interesting to recall the words Caiaphas spoke in the Sanhedrin, when they were plotting to kill Jesus: "You know nothing at all! You do not realize that it is better for you that one man die for the people than that the whole nation perish" (John 11:49-50). The apostle John comments: "He did not say this on his own.... He prophesied that Jesus would die for the Jewish nation, and not only for that nation but also for the scattered children of God, to bring them together and make them one" (John 11:51-52). Dix emphasizes that Caiaphas was alluding to "a piece of knowledge which the Council should have had in mind, but of which they were ignorant—some tradition or writing: his words would be an adequate summary of the passage in *T. Benjamin*, or of the tradition underlaying it, or to which it gave rise."[36]

Joseph and Aseneth

Joseph and Asenath[37] is a romantic story, written sometime in the period between the first century BCE and CE.[38] This work is clearly Jewish, developed from Gen 41:45, which states that Pharaoh gave Joseph a woman named Asenath, daughter of Potiphera, priest of On, to be his wife. This document was composed for Jews and perhaps for the *God-fearing* sympathizers who thought and lived in the Jewish ways,[39] since it assumes the reader knows the Jewish scriptures, as well as Jewish life and customs.[40] The marriage between the righteous Joseph and the pagan Asenath was problematic for strictly observant Jews, and this dilemma was also present in the author's own time with the attraction between the Jews and the proselytes.[41] Joseph's love story tries to address this concern.[42] Marc Philonenko suggests two tra-

---

[36] Ibid.

[37] In the Pseudepigrapha, Asenath of Genesis is referred to as Aseneth. This study uses Asenath when referring to the biblical text, but uses Aseneth when referring to the pseudepigraphical text.

[38] Rees Conrad Douglas, "Liminality and Conversion in Joseph and Aseneth," *JSP* 3 (1988): 34.

[39] An attempt to argue for Christian interpolation has been made. See Traugott Holtz, "Christliche Interpolation in Joseph und Aseneth," *NTS* 14 (1968): 482-97.

[40] C. Burchard, "Joseph and Aseneth: A New Translation and Introduction," in *The Old Testament Pseudepigrapha*, ed. James H. Charlesworth (New York: Doubleday, 1985), 2:195.

[41] Marc Philonenko, "Joseph and Asenath," *EncJud* 11:418.

[42] Ibid.

ditions were developed concerning Asenath's background.[43] One tradition states that she was the daughter of Dinah and Shekem (Tg. Ps.-J. Gen 41:45), and the other, which is the tradition presented in this document, claims that she was an Egyptian (Jos. Asen. 1:3-6).

The story of Joseph and Asenath is a lengthy footnote to the Joseph narrative and can be divided into two different episodes, chs. 1-21 and 22-29. The first episode alludes to Gen 41:46-49 and 41:50-52 and takes place in the house of Asenath's father. It tells about Joseph's and Asenath's sudden love, Asenath's conversion, and their marriage. The second episode alludes to Gen 41:53-54, 45:26-46:7, and 47:27 and takes place a few years later. In this part, Pharaoh's oldest son and a few of Joseph's brothers (the sons of Jacob's maidservants), conspire against Joseph, Asenath, and Pharaoh. Pharaoh's son wants to kill Joseph and his father, take the throne, and make Asenath his queen.[44] This coup d'état is thwarted by Leah's sons and Benjamin. The story concludes with: "And Pharaoh died at a hundred and nine years, and left his diadem to Joseph. And Joseph reigned as king in Egypt for forty-eight years, and after this he gave the diadem to Pharaoh's younger offspring, who was at the breast when Pharaoh died. And Joseph was like a father to Pharaoh's younger son in the land of Egypt all the days of his life" (Jos. Asen. 29:8-9).

Aseneth's description of Joseph when she saw him the first time is very fascinating. Joseph is pictured as a royal king and a son of God, and to him are attributed almost supernatural abilities.

> [5]And Joseph was dressed in an exquisite white tunic, and the robe which he had thrown around him was purple, made of linen interwoven with gold, and a golden crown (was) on his head. And around the crown were twelve chosen stones. And on top of the twelve stones were twelve golden rays. And a royal staff was in his left hand, and in his right hand he held outstretched an olive branch, and there was plenty of fruit on it, and in the fruit was a great wealth of oil.
>
> (Jos. Asen. 5:5)

---

[43] For further study about the two traditions, see V. Aptowitzer, "Asenath, the Wife of Joseph: A Haggadic Literary-Historical Study," *HUCA* 1 (1924): 239-306.

[44] Burchard, "Joseph and Aseneth," 182.

> ²ᵈAnd now, behold, the sun from heaven has come to us on
> its chariot
> and entered our house today,
> and shines in it like a light upon the earth.
> ... ³ᶜand did not know that Joseph is (a) son of God.
> ... ⁵And now, where shall I go and hide from his face
> in order that Joseph the son of God⁴⁵ does not see me
> ... ⁶And where shall I flee and hide,
> because every hiding place, he sees
> and nothing hidden escapes him,
> because of the great light that is inside him?
>
> (Jos. Asen. 6:2-6)

It is intriguing to note the parallel made between Joseph and Michael, the archangel of heaven. Aseneth saw "a man in every respect similar to Joseph, by the robe and the crown and the royal staff" (14:9). This man, like Joseph, also came from the east (5:2||14:1; 17:8)⁴⁶ and came riding in a chariot of four horses (5:4||17:8). Joseph is like Michael in that both are second in command, Michael in heaven and Joseph in Egypt. It could be argued that Joseph is presented as a type of Michael.

When Joseph came the second time to Aseneth's home, she had dressed herself in wedding garments and was waiting to lead him into her house and seat him on her father's throne. She had been transformed to the same glory as Joseph had as she prepared for the wedding (ch. 18), and when Joseph and Aseneth kissed each other for the first time, Joseph gave her the spirit of life, the spirit of wisdom, and the spirit of truth (19:10-11). It is important to note that these gifts did not come from God, but from Joseph himself. When Aseneth married Joseph, she became a queen (28:13) and an eternal city of refuge (15:7; 16:16; 19:5), a symbol of Zion, the City of God.⁴⁷

Would there be, by chance, a parallel between this love story and the love story between God and His virgin bride in the Hebrew Scripture, His

---

⁴⁵ Joseph is also called the "firstborn son" of God, both by Michael and his own brothers (18:11; 23:10).

⁴⁶ Burchard states in his commentary on Jos. Asen. 11:2 that the direction "east" may denote either that tradition or the direction of the rising sun as a symbol of God or new life (Burchard, "Joseph and Aseneth," 217).

⁴⁷ Ibid., 198.

pure people that He is waiting to marry, and His holy city? If so, Joseph would certainly fit the role as a type of God's Son within a Christian setting.

3 Enoch

3 Enoch is a Jewish book[48] claimed to be an account by Ishmael ben Elisha of his ascent to heaven. It describes what he saw on his journey and the revelations the archangel Metatron gave him. This noted Rabbi died shortly before the Bar Kokhba revolt, which broke out in 132 CE. P. Alexander notes that scholars differ regarding the dating, but they do agree that 3 Enoch was not written by Ishmael. He concludes that because "3 Enoch contains some very old traditions and stands in direct line with developments which had already begun in the Maccabean era, a date for its final redaction in the fifth or sixth century A.D. cannot be far from the truth."[49]

In the eschatological section of 3 Enoch, Ishmael is shown this world's history from Adam until the coming of the Messiah. One of the historical figures mentioned briefly is the Messiah ben Joseph. When only a brief description is casually mentioned in the text, one can reasonably assume the writer is referring to a tradition which was, at that point, well established and common knowledge. In 3 Enoch 45:5 the writer states:

> And I saw:
> the Messiah the son of Joseph and his generation, and all that they will do to the gentiles.
> And I saw:
> the Messiah the son of David and his generation, and all the battles and wars, and all that they will do to Israel whether for good or bad.
> And I saw:
> all the battles and wars which Gog and Magog will fight with Israel in the days of the Messiah, and all that the Holy One, blessed be he, will do them in the time to come.

---

[48] This document is also known as Seper Hekalot (The Book of the Palaces), The Chapter of Rabbi Ishmael, and The Book of Rabbi Ishmael the High Priest.

[49] P. Alexander, "3 (Hebrew Apocalypse of) Enoch: A New Translation and Introduction," in *The Old Testament Pseudepigrapha*, ed. James H. Charlesworth (New York: Doubleday, 1983), 1:223-29.

This study has, thus far, shown it is very likely the expectation of a Messiah ben Joseph was present in the pre-Christian era, perhaps as early as the third-century BCE, based on the blessings found in Genesis 49 and the prophetic words in Isa 52:13-53:12 and Zechariah 12. Even if 1 En. 90:37-38,[50] T. Naph. 5:1-8; Sib.Or 5.256-59; 4 Ezra 7.28-29; 4QTesimonia; 4Q372;[51] 4Q474[52] refer or allude to the Messiah ben Joseph, there is limited detailed information given about him in Second Temple period writings.[53] In Rabbinic Judaism, however, more details are provided.

Later Jewish Interpretation (Rabbinic Judaism)[54]

In Jewish writings dated after the destruction of Jerusalem, Messiah ben Joseph is the forerunner of the Messiah ben David. He will prepare the way for Messiah ben David and the messianic age, but he will fall in battle when fighting against Israel's enemies at the end-time. de Jonge speculates

---

[50] It could be argued that the "great beast with the huge black horns on his head" alludes to Deut 33:17. If so, then the Messiah (the beast) described in the Animal Apocalypse of 1 Enoch could refer to Messiah ben Joseph as proposed by Mitchell (*Messiah ben Joseph*, 61-72). Although Himmelfarb finds Mitchell's identification of "the white bull of the *Book of Dreams* as the firstling bull of Deut 33:17 and understands the transformed bull with the large black horns of the *Book of Dreams* as the horned wild ox of Deuteronomy" intriguing and plausible, she argues there is no hint of a sacrificial death of this bull in the Animal Apocalypse, nor is this bull called a firstling (a sacrificial bull). Thus, she concludes Mitchell's identification needs further exploration as it currently seems to go beyond "what the passage under discussion will support" (Himmelfarb, "Messiah Son of Joseph," 775-76).

[51] Mitchell discusses T. Naph. 5:1-8, Sib.Or 5.256-59, 4 Ezra 7.28-29, 4QTest, 4Q372, 4QMessAp and 11QMelch in *Messiah ben Joseph*, 67-69, 79-95. It should be noted that Himmelfarb finds no evidence for a Messiah ben Joseph in these texts and concludes: "in the absence of clear evidence to the contrary, the date of the earliest certain evidence for the idea of a messiah descended from Joseph, no earlier that the tannaitic period, should be understood as indicating the period in which the idea emerged" ("The Messiah Son of Joseph in Ancient Judaism," 789).

[52] See Torleif Elgvin, "4Q474 — A Joseph Apocryphon?" *RevQ* 18 (1997): 97-107, n.18.

[53] Although little has been written about Messiah ben Joseph and his mission, it could still be a part of the oral tradition.

[54] David Mitchell's book, *Messiah ben Joseph*, identifies many references in Rabbinic literature to Messiah ben Joseph and many of these references have been utilized in this study.

the belief in this warlike Messiah, who will die in the battle, arose after the defeat of Bar Kokhba.[55] Joseph Heineman states most scholars have overlooked the references to this Messiah in contexts unrelated to battle and defeat, suggesting the Messiah ben Joseph tradition could be older than the Bar Kokhba period.[56] In this period, the tradition that Esau would fall by the hand of Joseph also appeared, based on Deut 33:17 and Zech 9:9.[57]

Talmud

The first clear references to Messiah ben Joseph is found in three statements on a single page of the tractate *Sukkah* in the Babylonian Talmud[58]—they are the following:

> And the land shall mourn, every family apart; the family of David apart, and their wives apart (Zech. 12:12).... What is the cause of this mourning? — R. Dosa and the Rabbis differ on the point. One explained, The cause is the slaying of Messiah the son of Joseph; and the other explained, The cause is the slaying of the Evil Inclination. — It is well according to him who explained that the cause is the slaying of Messiah the son of Joseph, since that well agrees with the Scriptural verse, *And they shall look upon me because they have thrust him through, and they shall mourn for him as*

---

[55] Marinus de Jonge, "Messiah," *ABD* 4:787.

[56] Heineman, "Messiah of Ephraim," 344.

[57] Gen. Rab. 75:5 states: "'I have sojourned with Laban and stayed until now' — why 'stayed until now'? Because Esau's adversary had not yet been born ... 'Ox' — this is the Anointed for War, as it is said 'His firstling ox, majesty is his' (Deut 33:17), 'ass' — this is the King Messiah, as it is said 'Lowly, and riding upon an ass' (Zech 9:9)."

[58] There are two versions of the Talmud, the Palestinian and the Babylonian, and they were written in the period between 200 – 650 CE. Of the two, the Babylonian is preeminent and considered to be normative for rabbinic Judaism. The Talmud consists of the Mishnah and its own Gemara (commentary) to most of the tractates of the Mishnah. The Talmud contains a wealth of Jewish thought on a variety of subjects. "Instead of one set rule per topic, the Talmud presents a text of Mishnah with the spectrum of views, at times in conflict with each other, contributed by the rabbis who participated in the Gemara process" (Lee J. Gugliotto, *Handbook for Bible Study: A Guide to Understand, Teaching, and Preaching the Word of God* [Hagerstown, MD: Review & Herald, 1995], 238).

> *one mourneth for his only son* (Zech. 12:10), but according to him who explains the cause to be the slaying of the Evil Inclination, is this an occasion for mourning? Is it not rather an occasion for rejoicing? Why then should they weep?
>
> Sukkah 52A (TOP)

> Our Rabbis thought, The Holy One blessed be He, will say to the Messiah, the son of David (May he reveal himself speedily in our days!), '*Ask of me anything, and I will give it to thee*', as it is said, *I will of the decree etc. this day have I begotten thee, ask of me and I will give the nation for thy inheritance* (Ps. 2:7, 8). But when he will see the Messiah the son of Joseph is slain, he will say to Him, 'Lord of the Universe, I ask of Thee only the gift of life'. 'As to life', He would answer him, 'Your father David has already prophesied this concerning you', as it is said, He asked life of thee, thou gavest it him [even length of days for ever and ever] (Ps. 21:5).
>
> Sukkah 52A (BOTTOM)

> 'And the Lord showed me four craftsmen' (Zech. 2:3). Who are these 'four craftsmen'? — R. Hana b. Bizna citing R. Simeon Hasida replied: The Messiah the son of David, the Messiah the son of Joseph, Elijah and the Righteous Priest.
>
> Sukkah 52B

When reading these three passages from the Talmud, the expectation of a coming Messiah ben Joseph, his connection to the Hebrew scripture, and violent death are considered common knowledge; the author sees no need in arguing or supporting his statements. This indicates this belief existed and may have been commonly accepted before it was written down. However, the question about the dating of these passages are uncertain, even if R. Dosa is considered the author of the first statement above – on the Messianic interpretation of Zech 12.[59] The dominant view, as mentioned earlier, is that Mes-

---

[59] Joseph Klausner, *The Messianic Idea in Israel: From Its Beginning to the Completion of the Mishnah*, trans. W. F. Stinespring (New York: Macmillan, 1955), 490-91.

siah ben Joseph was invented following the failed Bar Kokhba revolt. However, the question of dating hinges on the identity of R. Dosa and how this statement relates to the immediate context.

Mitchell challenges the dominant view by making several pertinent observations. First, he notes these passages are multilayered – consisting of Bible text, and commentary both in Hebrew and Aramaic. He argues "Hebrew passages in the Talmud mostly record oral traditions which originated in the Holy Land before AD 200, while Aramaic passages date from after that time. So, in our present text, the Aramaic passages are redactoral comments on a Hebrew oral tradition."[60] Rabbi Dosa's words are recorded in Hebrew, suggesting a tannaitic origin. Second, he remarks the context of the debate is the scriptural justification for the alteration made to the Court of Women – thus the debate takes place prior to its destruction while the Feast of Sukkot was still celebrated, which suggests the debate could not have taken place after 66 CE when the celebration had ceased. Assuming R. Dosa refers to Dosa ben Harkinas, a second-generation Palestinian *tanna*, Mitchell postulates, "the outside dates for the debate are about AD 55 to 65."[61] Based on the casual way Messiah ben Joseph is mentioned in the discussion, it would be reasonable to assume he was already well established in Jewish traditions by the end of the Second Temple Period.

The second and third passage listed above are harder to date. The second passage is introduced by the phrase "our rabbis thought" which Mitchell suggests is significant as this phrase "introduces an anonymous tradition from before AD 200," a date which "is confirmed by the fact that the passage is in Hebrew, not Aramaic." The third passage regarding the identity of the four craftsmen is attributed to "the late second century *tanna*, R. Shimon, and his third century disciple, R. Hana" only suggests this "tradition existed in the late second century AD."[62] However, Mitchell argues this tradition of the four craftsmen can be traced back to the Qumran community 4Q175 indicating the antiquity of the Messiah ben Joseph or a Josephite Messiah.[63]

These three passages reveal that Zech 12:10 is associated with Messiah ben Joseph, he will be slain and his death seems to be related in some way to the slaying of the Evil Inclinations. According to the second passage, Messiah ben Joseph is the forerunner of Messiah ben David as the latter sees

---

[60] Mitchell, *Messiah ben Joseph*, 127.
[61] Ibid., 129.
[62] Ibid., 133.
[63] Ibid., 79-81, 133-36.

the former slain, he asks God to resurrect him, suggesting a larger tradition with an eschatological sequence of events. The third passage reveals that Messiah ben Joseph shares an eschatological role with three additional figures, Messiah ben David, Elijah, and the Righteous Priest, again suggesting a larger eschatological belief system.

Regardless of the dating given to these passages from the Talmud, it is important to remember that in the Second Temple period there were a great variety of messianic figures. David Flusser notes: "The Old Testament Book of Zechariah already makes mention of two Messianic figures, the high priest and the messianic king,"[64] and the Dead Sea Scrolls mention a third messianic person, the prophet of the Last Days. Flusser observes these three messianic figures are based "upon a broader ideological concept" in the scrolls as it "corresponds to the three main functions of the ideal Jewish state, in which Kingdom, priesthood, and prophecy shall exist (see 1 Macc. 14:41)."[65] It would not be unreasonable to assume that the concept of the Messiah ben Joseph also emerged during this period. One thing agreed upon by scholars is this belief, that a Messiah would come from the line of Joseph, has a Jewish origin.

Midrashim

There are several references to Messiah ben Joseph in the literature belonging to the Rabbinic genre of Midrash, which were compiled by a number of editors and authors, primarily between 400 and 1200 CE. Barry W. Holtz notes that "originally, midrashic literature was oral—sermons preached in the synagogues and teachings of various sages. During the years mentioned, Midrashim were edited, organized, and written down, but midrashic texts often represent traditions a good deal older than the period of the written books."[66] Midrashim interpret both legal (Midrash halacha) and non-legal/narrative literature (Midrash aggadah), noting that most works would easily be considered as homiletical or exegetical Midrash.[67] In Table 5,

---

[64] David Flusser, "Messiah: Second Temple Period," *EncJud* 14:111.

[65] Ibid.; see also Craig A. Evans, "Messiahs," *EDSS* 1:537-42; and Kenneth E. Pomykala, "Messianism," *Eerdmans Dictionary of Early Judaism*, ed. John J. Collins and Daniel C. Harlow (Grand Rapids: Eerdmans, 2010), 938-42.

[66] Barry W. Holtz, "Midrash," in *Back to the Sources: Reading the Classic Jewish Texts*, ed. Barry W. Holtz (New York: Simon & Schuster,1984), 178.

[67] Ibid., 186-88.

Table 5. Midreshei Aggadah according to types and periods

Aggadic Work	Midrashim	Date CE	Era
	Mekhilta Sifra Sifre	< 200	Tannaitic Period
	Genesis Rabbah *Leviticus Rabbah* Lamentations Rabbah Esther Rabbah I	400-500	Classic Amoraic Midrashim of the Early Period (400-600)
Apocalyptic and Eschatological Midrashim	*Pesikta de-Rav Kahana* Songs Rabbah Ruth Rabbah	500-640	The Middle Period (640-100)
Megillat Antiochus Midrash Petirat Moshe ("Death of Moses") Tanna de-Vei Eliyahu ("Seder Eliyahu") Pirkei de-R. Eliezer Midrash Agur (Called "Mishnat R. Eliezer") Midrash Yonah	*Targum Sheni* Midrash Esfah Midrash Proverbs Midrash Samuel Ecclesiastes Rabbah Midrash Haserot vi-Yterot	640-900	
Midrash Petirat Aharon Divrei ha-Yamim shel Moshe Otlyyot de-R. Akiva Midrash Sheloshah ve-Arba'ah Midrash Eser Galuyyot Midrash va-Yissa'u	*Deuteronomy Rabbah* *Tanḥuma* *Tanḥuma (Buber)* *Numbers Rabbah II* *Pesikta Rabbati* *Exodus Rabbah II* *Va-Yeḥi Rabbah* *The Manuscripts of the Tanḥuma* *Yelammedenu Midrashim*	(775-900)	
Throne and Hippodromes of Solomon Midreshel Ḥanukkah Midreshel Yehudith Midrash Hallel Midrash Tadshe	Midrash Tehillim I Exodus Rabbah I *Aggadat Bereshit* Aggadat Shir ha-Shirim (Zuta) Ruth Zuta Ecclesiastes Zuta Lamentations Zuta	900-1000	
Midrash Aseret ha-Dibberot Midrash Konen Midrash Avkir Alphabet of Ben Sira Midrash va-Yosha Sefer ha-Yashar	Midrash Shir Hashirim Abba Guryon Esther Rabbah II Midrash Tehillim II	1000-1100	The Late Period (1000-1200)
Pesikta Ḥadta Midrash Temura	Panim Aḥerim le-Esther (version 1) Lekaḥ Tov (c. 1110) Midrash Aggadah Genesis Rabbati Numbers Rabbah	1100-1200	
	Yalkut Shimoni	1200-1300	The Period of the Yalkutim (anthologies) 1200-1500
	Midrash ha-Gadol Yalkut Makhiri	1300-1400	
	Ein Ya'akov Haggadot ha-Talmud	1400-1500	

Source: Moshe David Herr, "Midrash," EncJud 14:184. The Midrashic texts from the Tannaitic period has been added to the table.

Moshe David Herr provides a list of midrashic works and their associated period, homiletical Midrashim are in italics while exegetical Midrashim are in regular font.

Mitchell suggests there are many references appearing in exegetical midrashim of "the conquering figure of the 'Anointed for war' or 'War Messiah' from Joseph and Ephraim," who, at times, is depicted "as a twosome with the King Messiah."[68] The most elaborate references to Messiah ben Joseph are found in *Pesikta Rabbati* 36-37 and in the apocalyptic Midrashim.

Pesiqta Rabbati

Pesiqta Rabbati is a collection of homilies originating in synagogues and schools, from "teachers of the second, third, fourth, or fifth generations of Palestinian Amoraim" (3rd–4th cent. CE), and was most likely redacted in the 7th century, although a 6th century dating is also possible.[69] Friedmann suggests pisḳah 36, *The light of the Messiah*, and pisḳah 37, *The ordeal and triumph of the Messiah*, which present the origin, suffering, and victorious Messiah ben Joseph, is of Tannaitic origin (2nd–3rd cent. CE), and as such, would predate the other Piskas. Braude, on the other hand, believes a post-Amoraic compilation (possibly in the 7th cent. CE) as more likely.[70]

Pisḳah 36 suggests God "contemplated the Messiah and his work before the world was created" (pisḳah 36.1; see also 33.6). This Messianic figure is named Ephraim Messiah, a likely synonym to Messiah ben Joseph. According to this homily, upon his creation, the Messiah was told about the suffering which was in store for him on the account of the people, and he accepted his destiny:

---

[68] Mitchell, *Messiah ben Joseph*, 142-43. He provides the following references to the war Messiah: Gen. Rab. 75.6; 99.2; Midr. Tanḥ 11.3; 'Ag. Ber. 63; 70; 79; Num. Rab. 14.1; Kuntres Acharon §20 to Yal. Shim. on the Pentateuch; Midr. Aleph Beth 11b.1-15; Pirqe R. El. 22a.ii; Tg. Ps.-J. to Exod 40:11; t. Tg. Zech 12.10; 'Ag. Mash. 20-24; Otot 5.7-8; 6.11-12; Sep. Zerub. 50 (after his resurrection); Pirqe Mash 5.45; Nistarot Rav Shimon ben Yoḥai 12; Tefillat Rav Shimon ben Yoḥai; Zohar Mishpatim, 478, 479; Abravanel, Commentary on Zech. 12:10. And the following references to a dual messiaship: Yal. Shim. §570 on Zech 4:3; Pesiq. Rab. 8.4; Midr. Tanḥ. 11.3; 'Ag. Ber. 63, 79.

[69] William G. Braude, ed., *Pesikta Rabbati: Discourses for Feasts, Fasts, and Special Sabbaths*, trans. William G. Braude, YJS 18 (New Haven: Yale University Press, 1968), 1:2-3, 20-26.

[70] Ibid., 1:22-23.

There are souls that have been put away with thee under My throne, and it is their sins which will bend thee down under a yoke or iron and make thee like a calf whose eyes grow dim with suffering, and will choke thy spirit as with a yoke; because of the sins of these souls thy tongue will cleave to the roof of thy mouth. Art thou willing to endure such things?

...

The Messiah will say: Master of the Universe, with joy in my soul and gladness in my heart I take this suffering upon myself, provided that not one person in Israel perish; that not only those who are alive be saved in my days, but that also those who are dead, who died from the days of Adam up to the time of redemption; and that not only these be saved in my days, but also those who died as abortions; and that not only these be saved in my days, but all those whom Thou thoughtest to create but were not created. Such are the things I desire, and for these I am ready to take upon myself [whatever Thou deceest].[71]

Piskah 36.2 and piskah 37.1-3 provide additional details regarding the time of the Messiah, his suffering, his glorification, his judgment, and the ultimate result of his redemptive act on behalf of God's people.

The Patriarchs will arise and say to the Messiah: Ephraim, our true Messiah, even though we are thy forbears, thou art greater than we because thou didst suffer for the iniquities of our children, and terrible ordeals befell thee, such ordeal as did not befall earlier generations or later ones; for the sake of Israel thou didst become a laughingstock and a derision among the nations of the earth; and didst sit in darkness, in thick darkness, and thine eyes saw no light, and thy skin cleaved to thy bones, and thy body was as dry as a piece of wood; and thine eyes grew dim from fasting, and thy strength was dried up like a potsherd—all these afflictions on account of the iniquities of our children, all these because of thy desire to have our children benefit by that goodness

---

[71] Ibid., 2:678-79.

which the Holy One, blessed be He, will bestow in abundance upon Israel....

The Patriarchs will say to him: Ephraim, our true Messiah, be content with thou has done, for thou hast made content the mind of thy Maker and our minds also.[72]

[All the nations] shall come and lick the dust touched by the feet of the king Messiah... And all of them shall come and fall upon their face before the Messiah and before Israel, and say: Let us be slaves unto thee and unto Israel. And each and every one in Israel will have two thousand and eight hundred slaves.[73]

Apocalyptic Midrashim

A more detailed description of Messiah ben Joseph and his eschatological role appears in apocalyptic Midrashim,[74] among which *Sefer Zerubbabel*[75] may be the best known. They follow the same general pattern, with variations in the finer details. Messiah ben Joseph (also known by the names Messiah ben Ephraim, Eprhaim ben Tsidqi, Ephraim Messiah, Nehemia ben Hushiel, and King Nehemiah Messiah in these midrashim), gathers an army to liberate Jerusalem, rules for a short period before he is slain and God's people flee to the desert. Following the appearance and the victory of Messiah ben David, Messiah ben Joseph is resurrected, either first or as a part of the general resurrection of the saints. Mitchell, provides an easy overview of

---

[72] Ibid., 2:685-86.

[73] Ibid., 2:682.

[74] *Aggadat Mashiaḥ, Otot Ha-Mashiaḥ, Asereth Otot, Pirqei Hekhalot Rabbati §38-40, Sefer Zerubbabel, Otot Rav Shimon ben Yoḥai, Pirqei Mashiaḥ, Nistarot Rav Shimon ben Yoḥai, Asereth Melakhim, Kitab 'al-'amanat wal-I'tiqadat*—by Sa'adya Gaon (ch. 7, section 5-6), *Midrash Vayosha on Exod 15:18*, and *Responsum on the Redemption*—by R. Ḥai ben Sherira Gaon. An additional apocalyptic midrash, *Tefillat Rav Shimn ben Yoḥai*, follows closely the other twelve midrashim, however, the text does not Messiah ben Joseph, although it mentions Nehemiah ben Hushiel who seems to parallel the biographical description of Messiah ben Joseph in the other midrashim. For a convenient anthology or excerpts of these apocalyptic midrashim, see Mitchell, *Messiah ben Joseph*, 151-217, 253-63.

[75] For a detailed analyze of *Sefer Zerubbabel*, see Martha Himmelfarb, *Martha. Jewish Messiahs in the Christian Empire: A History of the Book of Zerubbabel* (Cambridge: Harvard University Press, 2017).

these elements in each of the apocalyptic works, making the differences and similarities clear (see Table 6). It should be noted, Zech 12:10, 12 is used as a proof-text in several of these midrashim.

Table 6. The apocalyptic midrashim summarized

Midrash	Date	Name	Place of origin	Slain by	Place of slaying	Israel in desert	Raised	Bib. vv. Re MbJ
1. Aggadat Mashiaḥ	Talmud Period	MbJ	Midst of Galilee	Gog	Gate of Jerusalem	Yes	General resurrection	
2. Otot haMashiaḥ	620	MbJ = NbH	Warriors from Ephraim	Armilus	Gates of Jerusalem	Yes	Yes; First	
3. Asereth Otot	620-30	MbJ/bE = NbH	Warriors from Ephraim	Armilus	Jerusalem	Yes	Yes; First, by Holy One for MbD	
4. Pirqei Hekhalot Rabbati	620-30?	EMT≈ MbJ = NbH	Gathers Israel to Jerusalem	Shirvan of Persia	Body at Jerusalem Gate	Yes	Yes; NbH raised.	
5. Sefer Zerub.	c. 633	MbJ/bE = NbH	—	Armilus	Body at Jerusalem Gate		Yes; NbH raised.	
6. Otot R. Shim. b. Yoḥai	c. 650	MbJ = NbH	—	Armilus	Jerusalem	Yes	—	Zech 12:12
7. Pirqei Mashiaḥ	Late 7th C.	KNM ≈ EM	Gathers Israel to Jerusalem	Arabs	Jerusalem	Yes	Nehem. Yes	
8. Nistarot R. Shim. b. Yoḥai	c. 750	MbJ/bE	Goes to Jerusalem	Armilus	East Gate of Jerusalem	Yes	General resurrect.	Zech 12:10
9. Asereth Melakhim	c. 750?	MbJ	Upper Galilee	Gog	Jerusalem	Yes	General resurrect.	Zech 12:10
10. Sa'adya, Kitab	933	MbJ	Upper Galilee	Armilus	Jerusalem	Yes	Yes; First	Zech 12:10
11. Midrash Vay-osha	11th C.	MbJ	—	Armilus	Jerusalem		General resurrect.	Zech 12:10
12. R. Ḥai Respons.	Early 11th C.	MbJ	Upper Galilee	Armilus	Jerusalem	Yes	Yes; First	Zech 12:10
13. Tef. R. Shim. b. Yoḥai	11th C.	NbH	—	—	Jerusalem	Yes	—	

Source: Mitchell, *Messiah ben Joseph*, 218.

The following abbreviations appear in Table 6: Messiah ben Joseph (MbJ), ben Ephraim (bE), Eprhaim ben Tsidqi (EMT), Ephraim Messiah (EM), Nehemia ben Hushiel (NbH), King Nehemiah Messiah (KNM), Messiah ben David (MbD).

Medieval Jewish Literature

This section will consider Medieval Jewish Literature, concentrating on several prominent rabbis who wrote about Messiah ben Joseph between 900–1650 CE.

Sa'adiah ben Yoseph Gaon (892–942 CE)

Sa'adiah, in his treaty concerning the redemption in the *Book of Beliefs and Opinions* (*Kitab 'al-'Amanat*), follows the general narrative outline regarding Messiah ben Joseph found in the apocalyptic midrashim (see above) and provides a detailed discussion of that tradition. Sa'adiah suggests Messiah ben Joseph will be the forerunner of Messiah ben David and will appear in upper Galilee, gather a Jewish army, liberate Jerusalem from Roman occupation, and become a ruler "for a certain length of time." However, Armilus will wage war against him, conquer the city, "and subject its inhabitants to massacre, captivity, and disgrace." Messiah ben Joseph will be among the slain. Following this turn of events, the Jews will suffer great misfortune which will cause many to abandon their faith. It is during this period the prophet Elijah and Messiah ben David will appear to bring redemption to the people.[76] Sa'adiah states that Messiah ben Joseph will be resurrected first in the resurrection of the dead "by virtue of his being a righteous and well-tried servant of God."[77] However, Sa'adiah believes the appearance of the Messiah from the line of Joseph is not certain as it is dependent on a lack of repentance by the people. He states:

> "I mean whether we do not repent and the events associated with *Messiah descended from Joseph* come to pass, or we do repent and are able to dispense with them—*the Messiah descended from David* will manifest himself to us suddenly. Should there be, however, [in the second eventuality] a *Mes-*

---

[76] Sa'adya Gaon, *The Book of Beliefs and Opinions: Translated from the Arabic and the Hebrew by Samuel Rosenblatt*. YJS 1 (New Haven: Yale University Press, 1948), 304.

[77] Ibid., 309.

siah descended from Joseph who would precede him, he would serve as his herald and as one who puts the nation in proper condition and clears the way, as Scripture says: *Behold, I send My messenger, and He shall clear the way before Me* (Mal. 3:1)."[78]

Shlomo Yitzchaki (1040–1105 CE)

Shlomo Yitzchaki, more commonly known by the acronym Rashi, mentions Messiah ben Joseph explicitly in his commentary on the TaNaKh.[79] The first two references are found in his commentary on Isa11:13 and 24:18 and mention both Messiah ben Joseph and Messiah ben David who will not envy each other and are both depicted as warriors. Although these two passages are brief, they do reveal the joint work of these two Messianic figures and the order of their appearance, Messiah ben Joseph first, followed by Messiah ben David. It should also be noted the reference to the wars of Gog following the wars of the two Messiahs, which are in line with the tradition appearing in the Apocalyptic Midrashim mentioned above.

Isaiah 11:13	Rashi
And the envy of Ephraim shall cease, and the adversaries of Judah shall be cut off; Ephraim shall not envy Judah, nor shall Judah vex Ephraim.	**Ephraim shall not envy Judah:** The Messiah, the son of David, and the Messiah, the son of Joseph, shall not envy each other.

Isaiah 24:18	Rashi
And it shall come to pass, that he who flees from the sound of the fright shall fall into the pit, and he who ascends from within the pit shall be snared in the trap, for windows from above have been opened and the foundations of the earth have trembled.	**he who flees from the sound of the fright shall fall into the pit. etc.:** Whoever escapes the sword of the Messiah the son of Joseph shall fall into the sword of the Messiah the son of David, and whoever escapes from there shall be snared in the trap of the wars of Gog.

---

[78] Ibid., 301-2.

[79] The references used from Rashi's commentary are taken from A. J. Rosenberg. "The Complete Tanach with Rashi—Judaica Press," Chabad.org, http://www.chabad.org/library/bible_cdo/aid/63255/jewish/The-Bible-with-Rashi.htm.

The third and final reference appears in Rashi's commentary on Zech 12:10. Unlike his commentary on b. Sukkah 52a in which he follows R. Dosa who identifies the one slain in Zechariah with Messiah ben Joseph (see discussion above), Rashi identifies "the me" as the exiled Israelites who were slain by the gentile nations. However, he explicitly states the Sages believed this verse referred to the slain Messiah ben Joseph.

Zechariah 12:10	Rashi
And I will pour out upon the house of David and upon the inhabitants of Jerusalem a spirit of grace and supplications. And they shall look to me because of those who have been thrust through [with swords], and they shall mourn over it as one mourns over an only son and shall be in bitterness, therefore, as one is embittered over a firstborn son.	**a spirit of grace and supplications:** That it should come into their mind to supplicate Me, and they will be in My good graces. **a spirit:** Talant in Old French, a desire. **they shall look to Me because of those who have been thrust through:** Jonathan renders: And they shall supplicate Me because of their wanderings. And they shall look to Me to complain about those of them whom the nations thrust through and slew during their exile. **and they shall mourn over it:** Over that slaughter. **as one mourns over an only son:** As a man mourns over his only son. And our Sages expounded this in tractate Sukkah (52a) as referring to the Messiah, son of Joseph, who was slain.

Avraham ben Meir Ibn Ezra (1089–1164 CE)

In Ibn Ezra's commentary regarding the Joseph blessing in Genesis 49, he observed the following regarding the phrase "From thence" in v. 24, "The mighty One of Jacob alludes to the Lord. From the power that Joseph received from the Mighty One of Jacob he was able to become, and indeed became, 'the shepherd of the stone of Israel.'"[80] This suggests Ibn Ezra understood the "shepherd" and "stone" of Israel to be Joseph and not God, as many Christian scholars would argue.

---

[80] Ibn Ezra, *Ibn Ezra's Commentary on the Pentateuch: Genesis (Bereshit)*, trans. H. Norman Strickman and Arthur M. Silver (New York: Menorah Publishing, 1988), 444.

Ibn Ezra also understood the prophecy in Zech 12-13 as pointing to Messiah ben Joseph. He gives the following interpretation:[81]

Zechariah 12:10

And I will pour (Zech. 12.10) Pour the spirit of grace and supplication on the dwellers in Jerusalem, before this will happen to them. For Messiah ben Joseph will be killed. Then the fury of Ha-Shem will burn and he will destroy all the nations that comes against Jerusalem. And this is: *And they will look to me*: then all the nations will look to me to see what I will do to those who transpierced Messiah ben Joseph.

ושפכתי - חן רוח אשפוך ותחנונים על יושבי
ירושלם, טרם זה תעבור עליהם בתחלה
צרה, כי משיח בן יוסף יהרג, אז יכעס השם
וישמיד את כל הגוים הבאים על ירושלם,
וזהו והביטו אלי- אז יביטו כל הגוים אלי
לראות מה אעשה לאלה אשר דקרו משיח בן
יוסף

Zechariah 13:7

Sword (Zech. 13.7). And he prophesies also about the great wars which will be in all the earth at the death of Messiah ben Joseph. And the meaning of *my shepherd* (13.7) (is) every king of *goyim* which Ha-Shem has caused to rule over the earth; and he thinks of himself that he is *like God* (12.8). Therefore *And against the hero who is close to me...smite the shepherd* (13.7). Ha-Shem will cut off ever king and *his flock will be scattered*. And so it is written in the following parshah, *And Ha-Shem will be king over all the earth* (14.9)

חרב - ותנבא עוד על מלחמות רבות תהיינה
בכל הארץ במות משיח בן יוסף.
וטעם רועי – כל מלך מהגוים שהמשילו
השם על הארץ והוא חושב על עצמו שהוא
כאלהים, ועל כן גבר עמיתי הך את
הרועה, יכרית השם כל מלך ותפוצינה
צאנו, כן כתוב בפרשה האחרת הדבקה
בזאת, והיה ה' למלך על כל הארץ

Ibn Ezra also identifies Messiah ben Joseph or Ephraim in two additional passages—Ps 80:18 and Mal 3:1. In the latter passage, מַלְאָכִי, *my messanger*, who will prepare the way for the Lord is identified with Messiah ben Joseph, possibly based on the tradition that he will prepare the way for Messiah ben David and the victory of the Lord.

---

[81] Ibn Ezra's commentary on Zechariah is sourced from www.sefaria.org and English translation from Mitchell, *Messiah ben Joseph*, 225.

Psalm 80:18

The meaning of *Let Thy hand be upon the man at Thy right hand* [80.18] is, "Let Your help be upon the man of Your right hand." "The man of Your right hand" refers to "the stock which Thy right hand hath planted (verse 16)." The aforesaid is a metaphor. It (the stock or the vine) represents Israel or the messiah of the house of Ephraim.[82]

Malachi 3:1

Behold, I will send my messenger-angel. This is probably Messiah ben Joseph. *The Lord*—he is the glorious one, he is *the messenger-angel of the covenant.*[83]

David Kimhi (1160–1235 CE)

David Kimhi, more commonly known by the acronym Radak, questioned (like Rashi) the Messiah ben Joseph interpretation of Zech 12:10 although he acknowledges this was the traditional view. He supports his skepticism by noting that lack of references to Messiah ben Joseph in general.

> *"And they shall mourn for him,"* as a man that has only one son and he dies, or as a man whose firstborn dies. Our rabbies, of blessed memory, have interpreted this of Messiah, the son of Joseph, who shall be killed in the war. But I wonder, according to their interpretation, how he is here spoken of unconnectedly, without any previous mention at all.[84]

Moses ben Nahman (1194–1270 CE)

Nachmanides, better known by the acronym Ramban, could not resist the temptation to engage in Messianic calculations. He used the prophecies in the book of Daniel to pinpoint the end-time, when the Messiah ben Joseph would appear to prepare the way for Messiah ben David. According

---

[82] Abraham Ibn Ezra, *Rabbi Abraham Ibn Ezra's Commentary on Books 3-5 of Psalms: Chapters 73-150*, trans. and annotated H. Norman Stickman (New York: Touro College Press; Brighton, MA: Academic Studies Press, 2016), 98.

[83] The English translation of Ibn Ezra's commentary is sourced from Mitchell, *Messiah ben Joseph*, 226.

[84] David Kimchi, *Rabbi David Kimchi's Commentary upon the Prophecies of Zechariah*, trans. A. M'Caul (London: James Duncan, 1837), 155.

to his calculation, the end-time would start in 1358 CE and in 1403 CE; forty years later (influenced by the Exodus story) God's people would be peaceably settled in Israel under Messiah ben David.[85] Mitchell notes Ramban also refers to Messiah ben Joseph in his commentary on Exod 17 and Zech 12:

Exodus 17:9[86]

And behold all that Moses and Joshua did with them in former time, Messiah ben Joseph and his seed will also do to them. And that is why Moses persevered.	בראשונה עמהם משה ויהושע עשו כל והנה כן על, זרעם עם יוסף בן ומשיח אליהו יעשו בד משה התאמץ

Ramban's commentary on Zech 12:10-12 follows the traditional view, considering Messiah ben Joseph the subject of the prophecy, adding elements from the larger Messiah ben Joseph tradition.

> And the house of Israel will anoint for themselves a Messiah, as said above, and this will be Messiah ben Joseph. And he will conquer lands and kingdoms and will go to Jerusalem. And he will build it, as it is written, *Ha-Shem builds up Jerusalem; he gathers the exiles of Israel* (Ps. 147.2). But he will die in battle. And of him it is said, *In that day the mourning will be great in Jerusalem* (Zech. 12.11). And it is said, *They will look to him whom they have pierced* (Zech. 12.10). And after that will come the ordinary dispersed [of Israel] from among the people and they will set over themselves another king and he is Messiah ben David.[87]

Moshe ben Shem-Tov (c. 1240–1305 CE)

Moshe ben Shem Tov, also known as Moses de León was a Spanish Kabbalist and is considered the author or redactor of *Sefer Zohar* (The Book of Splendor), a foundational work for Kabbalistic thought or Jewish mysticism. The Zohar is a pseudepigraphical work which claims to derive from R.

---

[85] Joseph Sarachek, *The Doctrine of the Messiah in Medieval Jewish Literature* (New York: Hermon Press, 1968), 174-75.

[86] Rambam's commentary on Exod 17:9 is sourced from: www.sefaria.org. The English translation is by Mitchell, *Messiah ben Joseph*, 226.

[87] Mitchell, *Messiah ben Joseph*, 227.

Simeon ben Yoḥai, a 2nd century tannaitic sage from Galilee. This work contains several references to Messiah ben Joseph—not only to his death but, in some passages, to him not dying.[88]

Isaac ben Judah Abravanel (1437–1508 CE)

The following statement, together with Iben Ezra's, is very interesting from a Christian standpoint. Both show that the Rabbis also considered the prophecy in Zechariah as messianic. The only difference is that while the Rabbis understood it to refer to the Messiah ben Joseph, the disciples and Christian scholars applied it to Jesus, the Messiah ben Judah. Abravanel comments: "It is more correct to interpret the passage of Messiah, the son of Joseph, as our Rabbis, of blessed memory, have interpreted it in the treatise Sukkah, for he shall be a mighty man of valour of the tribe of Joseph, and shall at first be captain of the Lord's host in the war (namely, against Gog and Magog), but in that war shall die."[89]

Moses Alshech (1508–1593 CE)

Perhaps the most intriguing statement about Messiah ben Joseph among the Medieval Jewish literature is the one given by Moses Alschech. It states:

> I will do yet a third thing, and that is, that 'they shall look unto Me, 'for they shall lift up their eyes unto Me in perfect repentance, when they see Him whom they pierced, that is, Messiah, the Son of Joseph; for our Rabbis, of blessed memory, have said that He will take upon Himself all the guilt of Israel, and shall then be slain in the war to make an atonement in such manner that it shall be accounted as if Israel had pierced Him, for on account of their sin He has died; and, therefore, in order that it may be reckoned to them as a perfect atonement, they will repent and look to the blessed One, saying that there is none beside Him to forgive those that mourn on account of Him who died for their sin: this is the meaning of 'They shall look upon Me.'[90]

---

[88] For a discussion on the Messiah ben Joseph references in *Sefer Zohar*, see Mitchell, *Messiah ben Joseph*, 227-30.

[89] Baron, *Visions and Prophecies of Zechariah*, 441.

[90] Ibid., 442.

Due to the strong parallel between this statement and the Christian belief in Jesus, some scholars have drawn the conclusion that when a Rabbi refers to the title "Messiah ben Joseph" he really speaks of Jesus. These Christian scholars claim that, after the Bar-Kokhba revolt, the Rabbis tacitly accepted Jesus as the suffering Messiah, but used the name that he was commonly called in Galilee. They hoped that this would camouflage them from "the hatred and persecution of their own followers, or of their Roman masters."[91] This theory sounds appealing at first glance, but it is problematic. The first problem is the text is referring to Messiah ben Joseph and his activities as something that will take place in the future, rather than the past, which would have been expected if they were really alluding to Jesus. The second problem is the text is still asserting the Messiah will be slain in a war, possibly the same war as the other "Messiah ben Joseph" passages mentioned. The third problem is the "Christian" aspects of this text were all present before the Christian era, as discussed in the Early Jewish Interpretation section.

Bacharach, Naphtali ben Jacob Elchanan

Naphtali ben Jacob Elhanan proposes in his scholarly work, "Emek Hamelek" published in 1648, the heritage of Messiah ben Joseph. He also believed that the Messiah ben Joseph would be as real as the Messiah ben David.

> This Messiah will be of the tribe of Ephraim, and, indeed, of the seed of Jeroboam, the son of Nebat, and he will be descended from the son of this same Abia. This Messiah will be in the sight of God a good son, as it is said (Ps. ii, 7): 'Jehova has said to me, Thou art my son, this day have I begotten thee.'... The Messiah ben Joseph will be Joseph himself, just as David is the Messiah ben David (that is, just as David will at some time appear as Messiah ben David).[92]

---

[91] See ibid., 441-42, n. 2.

[92] Emek Hamelek, vol. 135, col. 1, ch. 18, quoted in Morton, "Doctrine of the Two Messiahs," 66.

The Figure of Joseph in Jewish Traditions

In the Second Temple period, Jewish literature began to explore the figure of Joseph. Joseph goes from receiving only scant attention outside the book of Genesis to becoming a prominent character. All of the writings consider him as a real person who became as powerful as the Hebrew scripture claims. He became an example of perfection for all to follow.[93] A larger body of tradition developed regarding the different aspects of Joseph's life story. They focused on his beauty, sexual temptations, his marriage to Asenath,[94] Joseph's change of heart towards his brothers, and the oath he asked of his brothers to take regarding his bones.[95] The special treatment of his body was regarded a mark of his greatness.[96] The Mishnah states: "Who is greater to us than Joseph, with whom none other than Moses concerned himself? Moses merited the bones of Joseph, and no one in Israel is greater than he" (m. Sotah 1.9).

Moses Aberbach notes the tradition that during the forty years of wandering in the wilderness, Joseph's bones were carried next to the Ark of the Covenant because Joseph had fulfilled all that was written in the Decalogue.[97]

Early Christian Period

Joseph was considered an example of humility, chastity, and prudent foresight by the early Church Fathers. They looked to Joseph as the highest ideal, a man who had lived what the gospel portrayed. Joseph was not only considered a prophet, but also as prophecy. Patrick Henry has observed that as early as Tertullian (c. 155 – c. 240 CE), the first Latin Church Father, Joseph was referred to as a figure of Jesus, and Cyprian (c. 200 – 258 CE), the leader of the Christian Church of Africa, called him a "type of Christ."[98] Some Fathers even saw Joseph as a symbol of Jesus' resurrection. Appendix 1 provides a list of some of the references to the Christological aspects of

---

[93] See, for instance, Harm W. Hollander, *Joseph as an Ethical Model*.

[94] See above discussion about *Joseph and Asenath*.

[95] See James L. Kugel, *In Potiphar's House: The Interpretive Life of Biblical Texts* (San Francisco: HarperCollins, 1990), and Moses Aberbach, "Joseph: In the Aggadah," *EncJud* 11:410-11.

[96] Patrick Reardon, "The Joseph Story: Narrative, Theology, & the Christian Hope," *Touchstone* 9 (1996): 29.

[97] Aberbach, "Joseph," 11:411.

[98] Reardon, "The Joseph Story," 28.

Joseph held by the early Church Fathers. Irenaeus (c. 130 – c. 202 CE) states the following about Christ: "From them Christ was foreshadowed and acknowledged and born; for in Joseph He was foreshadowed; from Levi and Judah He was born according to the flesh as king and priest; and through Simeon He was acknowledged in the temple."[99]

This comment by Irenaeus is very interesting in light of the above study of "the Lamb of God" in the *Testament of the Twelve Patriarchs*. It seems he adapted much of this view. He harmonized the expectation of a Messiah from Judah and one from Levi by arguing that Christ was an offspring from both of these two tribes. Instead of expecting a Savior to come from Joseph, as the Jewish tradition holds, he looked at Joseph as a type of the coming Messiah.

Patrick Reardon believes the tradition of reading the Joseph story during the Easter holiday in the Eastern Church might be the most significant indication that Joseph is considered as a type of Christ. He writes:

> The Eastern Church in particular has long read the Joseph story during Holy Week, a context highlighting so many resemblances of Joseph to Jesus: the beloved of his father, sold for a price by his brethren, unjustly accused and imprisoned on false testimony, suffering all with patience, and finally showing mercy towards his oppressors. Joseph's life thus outlined those dramatic days culminating on Calvary. Such is the contemplative vision enshrined forever in the Matins Bridegroom Service of Holy Week in the Orthodox Church: "Joseph is an image of the Master: he was thrown into a pit and sold by his brethren, but he suffered all these things with patience, as a true figure of Christ."[100]

Joseph was considered as a type of Jesus by the Church Fathers as well as the following generations of Christian theologians. They all assumed that Joseph was a historical person and that blessings in Gen 49 were given by Jacob. It

---

[99] Iren, Fragm. Xvii. (ed. Harvey, ii. 487), quoted in William J. Deane, *Pseudepigrapha: An Account of Certain Apocryphal Sacred Writings of the Jews and Early Christians* (Edinburgh: T&T Clark, 1891), 165.

[100] Reardon, "The Joseph Story," 28.

was not until the Enlightenment and the emergence of the Historical Critical Method that these views were challenged.[101]

The Enlightenment/Historical-Critical Method

At the advent of the Historical Critical Method, many scholars discarded the traditional view of Jacob's and Moses' blessings on the tribes. Instead of considering the blessings as a prophecy or prediction delivered by Jacob and Moses pointing forward to the Messianic age, they developed at least four other theories. None of the four theories consider the blessings to be prophetic. The first theory, which is the most prominent, considers them to be tribal blessings that do not have any literary connection with each other, they are not really a part of the Pentateuchal narrative, and were developed at different times. This theory also suggests it was a redactor in the sixth or fifth century who put them together.[102] The second theory suggests they have a political connotation and reflect the political climate at the time of the kings. Genesis 49 reflects the southern perspective, while Deut 33 reflects the northern perspective—one focuses on Judah, while the other focuses on Joseph (Ephraim).[103] The third theory asserts the blessings refer to the tribes' location in Egypt.[104] The fourth theory assumes the blessings refer to the time period when the tribes were settling in Palestine.[105] Stanley Gevirtz has tried to give the Joseph blessing (Gen 49:22) a geopolitical explanation, but this theory is not listed in addition to the four theories above since it has not been applied to all the blessings.[106]

Summary

There is sufficient evidence to support the expectation of a Savior from the tribe of Joseph was a pre-Christian idea, which was developed more fully in Rabbinic Judaism. The anticipation of the Messiah ben Joseph was built on an exegesis of the Jewish scripture which used passages such as Gen 49, Deut 33, Isa 52-53, and Zech 12. It could therefore be argued that the

---

[101] Heck, "Genesis 49 and Deuteronomy 33," 17.

[102] Ibid., 17-18.

[103] Ibid., 18-19, 22.

[104] Cope Whitehouse, "The Bahr Jūsuf and the Prophecy of Jacob," *PSBA* 8 (3 November 1885): 6-25, 57-59.

[105] Heck, "Genesis 49 and Deuteronomy 33," 25.

[106] See Stanley Gevirtz, "Of Patriarchs and Puns: Joseph at the Fountain, Jacob at the Ford," *HUCA* 46 (1975): 33-54.

Jewish people were waiting for a suffering Messiah before the advent of Christianity. The Joseph narrative was considered as a historical event and the blessing given by Jacob and Moses as a prophecy pointing forward to the messianic age.

The Early Church may have adopted the, possibly established, Jewish belief in a suffering Savior rather than the reverse. Instead of accepting the belief in a Messiah ben Joseph, they applied the scriptural evidence to Jesus Christ while arguing that Joseph foreshadowed Jesus. Joseph was referred to as a "type of Christ" because of the perfect life he lived and the similarities between his and Jesus' life. The Early Church Fathers also considered Joseph as a real person and the blessings as a historical event.

2. Translation and Notes on the Joseph Oracle

The Joseph oracle in Gen 49:22-26 is one of the more difficult passages in the Hebrew Scriptures. In the literary analysis of this oracle, some possible translations are presented. However, this passage has too many complex technicalities for all translations to be considered in depth in this study. Thus, in this instance, only the most prevalent are discussed, and the following single translation does not lay any claim to certainty, it merely presents one translation out of many.[1]

A Possible Translation

²² Joseph is a son of fruitfulness,	²² בֵּן פֹּרָת יוֹסֵף
a son of fruitfulness at the spring	בֵּן פֹּרָת עֲלֵי־עָיִן
—daughters [or his offspring] run over the wall	בָּנוֹת צָעֲדָה עֲלֵי־שׁוּר:
²³ The owners of arrows [archers] sorely grieved him, shot at him, and hated him.	²³ וַיְמָרֲרֻהוּ וָרֹבּוּ וַיִּשְׂטְמֻהוּ בַּעֲלֵי חִצִּים:
²⁴ But his bow remained strong, and the arms of his hands were made flexible by the hands of the mighty one of Jacob	²⁴ וַתֵּשֶׁב בְּאֵיתָן קַשְׁתּוֹ וַיָּפֹזּוּ זְרֹעֵי יָדָיו מִידֵי אֲבִיר יַעֲקֹב
From there, the shepherd, the stone of Israel	מִשָּׁם רֹעֶה אֶבֶן יִשְׂרָאֵל:

---

[1] For a detailed study of the Joseph oracle, see James R. Battenfield, "Hebrew Stylistic Development in Archaic Poetry: A Textual-Critical and Exegetical Study of the Blessing of Jacob, Genesis 49:1-27" (PhD diss., Grace College, 1976), Helmuth Pehlke, "An Exegetical and Theological Study of Genesis 49:1-28" (PhD diss., Dallas Theological Seminary, 1985), and Martin Rösel, "Die Interpretation von Genesis 49 in der Septuaginta," *BN* 79 (1995): 54-70.

²⁵ From the God of your father who helps you, and Shaddai who blesses you
with blessings of heaven above
blessings of the deep that lie below
blessings of the breasts and womb
²⁶ The blessings of your father have prevailed above
   the blessings of my progenitors
unto the desire of the everlasting mountains
They shall be on the head of Joseph
   and on the crown of the prince among his brothers.

²⁵ מֵאֵל אָבִיךָ וְיַעְזְרֶךָ
וְאֵת שַׁדַּי וִיבָרְכֶךָּ
בִּרְכֹת שָׁמַיִם מֵעָל
בִּרְכֹת תְּהוֹם רֹבֶצֶת תָּחַת
בִּרְכֹת שָׁדַיִם וָרָחַם:
²⁶ בִּרְכֹת אָבִיךָ גָּבְרוּ עַל־בִּרְכֹת הוֹרַי
עַד־תַּאֲוַת גִּבְעֹת עוֹלָם
תִּהְיֶיןָ לְרֹאשׁ יוֹסֵף וּלְקָדְקֹד נְזִיר אֶחָיו:

Literary Analysis

V. 22: Rashbam (1080?–1174 CE) suggests verse 22a is an example of "ladder" parallelism.[2] The "ladder" consists of two lines in which the second line completes the statement given in the first.[3]

Son of fruitfulness: The phrase בֵּן פֹּרָת is a difficult phrase since the feminine form of פרה does not appear in the Hebrew Scripture. This may be why commentaries often translate this verse differently. The two most prevalent interpretations compare Joseph to a wild ass at a spring[4] or a fruit tree at a well.[5] The present translation takes a third position, that the parallelism is a reference to Joseph as the son of fruitfulness, which is based on the root פרה, meaning "to be fruitful."

The remaining part of the verse is affected by the interpretation of the first part. If one compares Joseph to an ass, the second half of the verse is translated "wild colts on a hillside." If compared to a fruit tree, the meaning changes to "the tendrils extend over the wall." Whatever the preferred trans-

---

[2] Rashban gives the following examples of "ladder" parallelism from the Hebrew Scripture, see Exod 15:6; Pss 92:10; 93:3; 94:3; Eccl 1:2.

[3] Martin I. Lockshine, *Rabbi Samuel Ben Meir's Commentary on Genesis: An Annotated Translation*, Jewish Studies 5 (Lewiston, NY: Mellen, 1989), 375.

[4] The imagery of an ass is very similar to one used for Joseph in Deut 33:17, where Joseph is likened to an ox—both being agricultural beasts of burden.

[5] The imagery of a fruit tree or a vine is used in other poetic passages in the Hebrew Scripture to describe a righteous person, like in Ps 1:3 and Jer 17:8. Joseph seems to fit this picture perfectly.

lation, Joseph is portrayed as a very prosperous person, who has everything he needs.

V. 23: Joseph's prosperity cultivated enemies. These enemies hated him, not just passively, but the verb שטם implies an active hatred which is manifested in persecution. Joseph's enemies actually wanted to kill him. Pehlke notes that בַּעֲלֵי חִצִּים is a *hapax legomenon* which could translate as "the Lords of arrows." The plural form might suggest Jacob was contemplating his sons' attack on Joseph. It could also be a representation of all the attacks Joseph endured in his lifetime. Arrows in biblical symbolism often refer to a verbal attack (Ps 64:3; Prov 25:18; Jer 9:3, 8), and in that sense the verse may be alluding to the slander and accusations of Potiphar's wife. This verse could also be pointing forward to either a future attack on an individual or the whole "tribe of Joseph."

V. 24: A question that needs to be considered when translating this verse is: Whose bow is described? The above interpretation assumes the bow belongs to Joseph since the noun is in the singular and has the pronoun suffix "his." From this, Joseph is fighting off his enemies with the help of God's power. Some scholars, on the other hand, assume the singular form is used collectively or distributively,[6] and refers to Joseph's enemies. This view is supported by the LXX which reads ותשב, "it was broken," implying the bow was broken. If this is the case, then the crushed bow belongs to the "Lords of arrows" from the previous verse. The Hebrew word באיתן would then be translated "rigid, inflexible" and ויפזו זרעי ידיו, "their arms were unsteady."[7]

Whether or not the bow belongs to Joseph, the primary purpose of the verse is to emphasize that God helped Joseph in the difficult position described in v. 23.

From there: The literal meaning of מִשָּׁם is "from there." Gordon Wenham notes that "many commentaries suggest that at this moment Jacob pointed up to heaven to indicate the source of the blessing."[8] This phrase could also be referring to the general place(s) where attacks was/were made on Joseph (v. 23), or to God's hands in the previous line. Robert Alter, in his commentary, repoints this phrase and translates it "through the name."[9] This

---

[6] See, for instance, E. A. Speiser, *Genesis*, AB 1 (Garden City, NY: Doubleday, 1987), 368-69.

[7] Ibid.

[8] Gordon J. Wenham, *Genesis 16-50*, WBC 2 (Dallas: Word, 1994), 486.

[9] Robert Alter, *Genesis: Translation and Commentary* (New York: Norton, 1996), 299.

clause could be understood to be pointing to Joseph, if translated parenthetically. This rendering "applies to Joseph the titles of 'shepherd' and 'stone of Israel'."[10] The phrase "from there" would then have the meaning "from Joseph." The interpretation of this clause will be looked at later.

The shepherd: A shepherd is a common image of God in Hebrew poetry and could be used as a divine title (see Gen 48:15; Pss 23:1; 80:1; Isa 40:11).

The stone: Nahum Sarna states the word "stone" is "nowhere else used as a divine name or in association with God."[11] This has led some scholars to translate the word as "rock," which is a familiar term for God, although this translation cannot be supported by the Hebrew text.

If keeping to the literal translation of אֶבֶן, there are two ways to understand the English word "stone." The first focuses on the usage of אֶבֶן in the Joseph narrative. It is a possibility that "stone" might have been an ancient title for God that disappeared early from the Hebrew language.[12] This title could have originated from Jacob's Bethel experience, when God appeared to Jacob and promised him protection and reassurance that Abraham's promises would be fulfilled through him (Gen 28:18-22). John G. Hale writes, "the stone which pillowed his [Jacob's] head during that memorable vision was set up for a memorial pillar, and consecrated with oil to be henceforth God's House."[13] Jacob also set up a stone when he met God at this place for a second time–when God also told Jacob that kings would come from his descendants (Gen 35:1-15).

The second way to understand the English word 'stone' considers the usage of אֶבֶן in poetry,[14] which has a rather thought-provoking meaning. This word is used within the context of building—often in connection with a form of support or a cornerstone. The poetry of Ps 118:22; Isa 8:13-17; 28:6; and Dan 2:34, 35, 45 uses "stone" as a figurative reference or prophecy of the coming Messiah. Thus, this could render the intriguing translation, "from Joseph, God, the Messiah."

---

[10] Herbert E. Ryle, *The Book of Genesis* (Cambridge: Cambridge University Press, 1921), 437.

[11] Sarna, *Genesis*, 344.

[12] Ibid.

[13] John G. Hale, "Exegesis of Genesis XLIX, 22-26," *ACQ* 17 (1875): 510.

[14] This second understanding was adopted by the New Testament writers and Jesus, and the phrase was used to support Jesus' messianic claim as seen in Matt 4:6; 21:42-46; Eph 2:20; and 1 Pet 2:4-10.

Ben Meir interprets the verse this way: "God who has been Israel's shepherd ('avir) and who shepherds me to this day, by sustaining me in Egypt through your greatness. THERE, (i.e. in Egypt,) God made you THE SHEPHERD OF 'even yisra'el—Israel's family."[15]

Vv. 25-26a: The last two verses of the blessing of Joseph show an abundance of blessings that were given to Joseph. The blessings concern all phases of life: Joseph's land, offspring, and animals. Jacob claims the blessings he gave to Joseph surpass the blessings his ancestors received.

Blessings of my progenitors: Gary Rendsburg suggests there is a Janus Parallelism in Gen 49:26a.[16] Cyrus Gordon gives the following explanation of this type of parallelism: "One kind of parallelism is quite ingenious, for it hinges on the use of a single word with two entirely different meanings: one meaning paralleling what precedes, and the other meaning what follows."[17]

The Janus Parallelism can be seen only if the vowel pointing is omitted from the Hebrew text. The phrase הורי עד could be "translated both 'my progenitors of old' (when pointed הוֹרַי עד as in MT) and 'mountains of old' (when pointed הָוְרֵי עד). Its familial connotation resumes אביך in the first stich and its topographic connotation anticipates גבעת in the third stich."[18] The *Targum Onkelos* and various English translations recognize the first meaning, whereas the LXX follows the second meaning. The *Targum Pseudo-Jonathan* has tried to combine the two meanings in its translation. It states:

> May the blessings of your father be added to the blessings wherewith Abraham and Isaac who are like mountains blessed you, and to the blessings of the four mothers who are like hills, Sarah and Rebekah, Rachel and Leah.[19]

From this, one could argue that Joseph received the sum of all the blessings given to the Patriarchs and the Matriarchs.

---

[15] Lockshine, *Rabbi Samuel Ben Meir's Commentary on Genesis*, 381.

[16] Gary A. Rendsburg, "Critical Notes: Janus Parallelism in Gen 49:26," *JBL* 99 (1980): 291.

[17] C. H. Gordon, "New Directions," *Bulletin de l'Académie imp. des Sciences de St. Petersbourg* 15 (1978), 59; quoted in Gary Rendsburg, "Critical Notes," 291.

[18] Rendsburg, "Critical Notes," 291.

[19] Ibid., 292.

V. 26b, the prince among his brothers: The word נָזִיר appears for the first time in the Hebrew Scripture in this verse. Apart from its use in connection with Joseph in this verse and in Deut 33:16, this noun carries the meaning of being consecrated or devoted to God (Num 6:2; Judg 13:5, 7, 17; 16:17; and Lam 4:7). When applied to Joseph there is no indication that Joseph made a Nazarite vow with God. It is possible to argue that the Hebrew word could be translated "the one who has separated from his brothers," but another option is to render it as "king" or "prince." Ben Meir translates this phrase as "A king over his brothers,"[20] and Lockshin emphasized that "nazir as a king is adumbrated in the Jerusalem Targum."[21] It is this royal aspect that is developed further in Deut 33:17.

Contextual Analysis
The Immediate Context

Table 7 shows the twelve oracles given by Jacob on his deathbed and demonstrates how the Joseph oracle fits into Genesis 49. It also displays the mother of each of the brothers, the meaning of their names, the reference to their birth, the order in which they were blessed, the symbol used for them in the blessings, and the scriptural reference for each blessing.

---

[20] Lockshine, *Rabbi Samuel Ben Meir's Commentary on Genesis*, 384.
[21] Ibid., n. 2.

Table 7. The oracles in Genesis 49

Mother	Son	Meaning of name	Reference of birth (Genesis)	Order of blessing	Symbol of blessing	Reference of blessing (Genesis)
L E A H	Ruben	Behold, a son	29:32	1	Reckless	49:3-4
	Simeon	Hearing	29:33	2	Violence	49:5-7
	Levi	Attachment	29:34	3	Violence	49:5-7
	Judah	Praise	29:35	4	Lion	49:8-12
B I L H A H	Dan	Judgment	30:6	7	Serpent	49:16-18
	Naphtali	Wrestle	30:8	10	Doe	49:21
Z I L P A H	Gad	Good Fortune	30:11	8	Raider	49:19
	Asher	Happy	30:13	9	Rich food	49:20
L E A H	Issachar	Reward	30:18	6	Donkey	49:14-15
	Zebulun	Abode	30:20	5	Ships	49:13
R A C H E L	Joseph	May he add	30:24	11	Fruitful	49:22-26
	Benjamin	Son of the right hand	35:18	12	Wolf	49:27

Source: John H. Walton, *Chronological and Background Charts of the Old Testament* (Grand Rapids: Zondervan, 1994), 18.

As shown in the table, it becomes apparent that the blessings were not given to the sons in the order of their birth. The first four sons and the last two are in chronological birth order, while the six central sons are not. The sons are blessed in the following order: (1) all the sons who were born to

Leah, (2) the sons born to Leah by her maidservant Zilpah and Rachel by her maidservant Bilhah, (3) the sons born to Rachel. This gives the following chiastic structure (see Fig. 1):

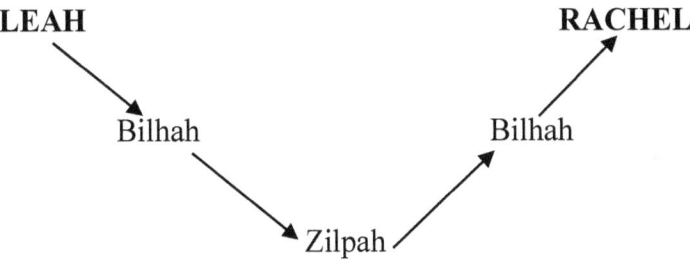

Fig. 1. The chiastic structure of Genesis 49. It is structured according to the order Jacob blessed his sons, and is based on Sarna's observations of the chapter. See Nahum M. Sarna, *Genesis*, The JPS Torah Commentary (Philadelphia: Jewish Publication Society, 1989), 331.

Outline of the Joseph Narrative

Table 8 lists the ten sections found in Genesis where the word *tōlĕdôt* appears in the Hebrew Scripture. The last of these ten introduces the generations of Jacob and Joseph in which Joseph is the central character. It is no wonder this whole section has been named the *Joseph Narrative*.

Although Joseph is the main figure in this narrative, "there are parts where he is not mentioned at all, or if he is mentioned, he is offstage."[22] In fact, the Joseph narrative is the first account in the Hebrew Bible that switches between two story lines: one follows Joseph, while the other follows Joseph's family. Figure 2 shows the interrelations of the Joseph story with Jacob and his family.

---

[22] Robert E. Longacre, *Joseph: A Story of Divine Providence, A Text Theoretical and Textlinguistic Analysis of Genesis 37 and 39-48* (Winona Lake, IN: Eisenbrauns, 1989), 22.

Table 8. The *tōlĕdôt* of Genesis

Section	The *tōlĕdôt* of Genesis	Scripture Reference
Unmarked*	Account of the creation of the heaven and the earth	1:1-2:3
1	The generation of heaven and earth	2:4-4:26
2	Book of generations of Adam	5:1-6:8
3	Generations of Noah	6:9-9:26
4	Generations of sons of Noah	10:1-11:9
5	Generations of Shem	11:10-11:9
6	Generations of Terah	11:10-26
7	Generations of Ishmael	11:27-25:11
8	Generations of Isaac, son of Abraham	25:12-18
9	Generations of Esau	36:1-37:1
10	These are the generations of Jacob	37:2-50:26

*The word *tōlĕdôt* is not used to introduced the creation account in the Hebrew text.

Robert E. Longacre has observed two macro-structures in this narrative, one more prominent than the other. The first deals with divine providence and has been summarized by Longacre in the following way: "Joseph's brothers, meaning to harm him sold him into Egypt, but in reality God sent him there so that he could save Jacob's family and many others from death by starvation."[23]

The author of the Joseph narrative emphasizes that God was with Joseph and turned Joseph's "misfortune" to something good. It is interesting to note that it is at Joseph's darkest hour, episodes 2 and 3, when God's name YHWH occurs. These two episodes are the only times when God's personal name is used in the entire narrative. This portrays a God who is loving, caring, and shows attention to individuals, especially when a person is most vulnerable.

The second structure, less prominent, deals with the preeminence of Judah and Joseph. It suggests they are destined to have leadership over Israel. As shown in Figure 2 and when reading the narrative, it becomes apparent

---

[23] Longacre, *Joseph*, 43.

2. Translations and Notes on the Joseph Oracle

	1	2	3	4	5	6	7	8	9	10	11	12	13	14
	37	38	39:1-6	39:7-23	40	41	42	43-45	46:1-47:12	47:13-31	48	49:1-28	49:29-50:21	50:22-26
	Episode 1		Episode 2	Episode 3	Episode 4	Peak	Interpeak	Peak	Post Peak 1	Post Peak 2	Post Peak 3			
Joseph														
Jacob and his family	Joseph sold into Egypt	Judah and Tamar	Joseph in Potiphar's house	Joseph's ruin	Prisoners' dreams	Pharaoh's dreams, Joseph's rise to power	Brothers' first trip to Egypt	Brothers' second trip to Egypt, Joseph reveals who he is	Jacob goes to Egypt	Last years of Joseph's famine administration	Joseph and the dying Jacob. Blessing of Manasseh and Ephraim	Blessings given to the Twelve Tribes	Death and burial of Jacob	Death of Joseph
Comments						Climax of the Joseph narrative		Denouement of Joseph						
Peaks												Peak of *tōlēdōt*		

Fig. 2. Interrelations of the Joseph story with Jacob and his family. Modified and reconstructed from: Longacre, *Joseph*, 22-23.

that Jacob, Judah, and Joseph are of primary interest to the author. This is also seen when reading Gen 49, where almost half the oracle concentrates on Judah and Joseph. Longacre claims the Jacob oracles are intended to be the high point of the Joseph narrative, if not of the whole book of Genesis.[24] He states that "among the descendants of Jacob, Joseph and Judah are to be preeminent both as individuals and as tribes."[25]

Certainly, the outline of the Joseph story indicates that the Joseph oracle is located in the most important chapter in the narrative and in the whole book of Genesis. Clearly, Gen 49 was the author's main focus.

Literary Pattern of the Pentateuch and the Joseph Story

John Sailhamer has identified several major poetic texts throughout the Pentateuch narrative, the most notable being Gen 49:1-27, Exod 15:1-17, Num 23:7-10, 18-24; 24:3-9,15-24, and Deut 32-33. He argues that a close study of the use of narrative and poetry sheds considerable light on the final shape of the work. Sailhamer states: "The technique of using a poetic speech and a short epilogue to conclude a narrative is well known in biblical literature and occurs frequently within recognizable segments of the Pentateuch itself."[26] Figure 3 shows the pattern found in Pentateuch:

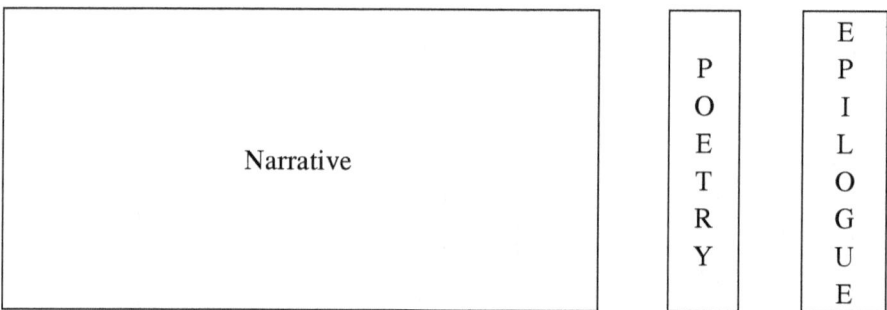

Fig 3. The literary pattern in the Pentateuch. Taken from Sailhamer, *Pentateuch as Narrative*, 35.

The above pattern can be found throughout the Pentateuch on different narrative levels. This suggests that it is an important part of the composi-

---

[24] Ibid., 23, 54.

[25] Ibid., 54.

[26] John H. Sailhamer, *The Pentateuch as Narrative: A Biblical-Theological Commentary*, Library of Biblical Interpretation (Grand Rapids: Zondervan, 1992), 35.

tional technique of the author. Figure 4 lists the pattern at the micro-structural level found by Sailhamer in the Prologue (Gen 1-11).[27]

	Narrative	Poetry	Epilogue
Creation	Gen 1:1-2:22	Gen 2:23	Gen 2:24
Fall	3:1-13	3:14-19	3:20-24
Cain	4:1-22	4:23	4:24-26
Genealogy	5:1-28	5:29	5:30-32
Flood Story	6:1-9:24	9:25-27	9:28-29

Fig. 4. The Narrative-Poetry-Epilogue pattern on the micro-structural level

Given this, it is no surprise that this pattern also occurs in the Joseph narrative. See Figure 5.

Narrative	Poetry	Epilogue
Gen 37-48:14	Gen 48:15-16, 20	48:20d-22

Fig.5. The Narrative-Poetry-Epilogue pattern in the Joseph narrative

Sailhamer notes this pattern also exists on the macro-structural level. The literary pattern with its poetic seams is what holds the Pentateuch together. The macro-structural level can be divided into four major narrative blocks, in which Jacob, Moses, Balaam, and Moses are the key figures in their respective poetic sections. Figure 6 shows the four major components in the higher level—the Patriarchal Narrative (Gen 12-50), the Exodus Narrative (Exod 1-15), the Wilderness Narrative (Exod 16 – Num 25), and the Moses Narrative (Num 26 – Deut 31). The third narrative block, the Wilderness Narrative, is interrupted by the Book of Leviticus as indicated by Part A and Part B in Figure 6, with the Book of Leviticus depicted as a triangle due to its chiastic structure.

William H. Shea notes the Book of Leviticus contains an overall chiastic structure in which Lev 16 serves as its central focus.[28] Based on his observations, the following chiastic structure appears: Sanctuary Legislations

---

[27] Idem., *The Meaning of the Pentateuch: Revelation, Composition and Interpretation* (Downers Grove, IL: InterVarsity Press, 2009), 34.

[28] William H. Shea, "Literary Form and Theological Function in Leviticus," in *70 Weeks, Leviticus, Nature of Prophecy*, ed. Frank B. Holbrook, DARCOM 3 (Washington, DC: Biblical Research Institute, General Conference of Seventh-day Adventists, 1986), 131-68.

(A – Lev 1-7 ‖ A' – Lev 24-27), Priestly Legislations (B – Lev 8-10 ‖ B' – Lev 21-23), Personal Legislation (C – Lev 11-15 ‖ C' – Lev 17-20), and the Day of Atonement (D – Lev 16) as the literary center. Wilfried Warning reaches the same conclusion through his analysis of the 37 divine speeches contained in Leviticus, noting that Leviticus 16 seems to serve both as the theological and structural center, supported on both a macro- and micro-structural level.[29]. Ángel Rodríguez suggests there is also a chiastic structure in Leviticus 16 itself, where the atoning sacrifice serves as the central element: G – Make atonement (Lev 16:16-19) and G' – Atonement is finished (Lev 16:20a).[30]

The central climatic position of the Day of Atonement and the atoning death on behalf of the people, is a central element from a typological redemptive perspective. It is located at the center of the final redaction of Pentateuch which introduces the two-trees and concludes with the two-ways, revealing the reward for obedience and the consequences of disobedience – expulsion and death (Gen 2:17; 3:2-5, 19b, 23-24—expulsion from the Garden of Eden and death ‖ Deut 27-30—covenant curses, expulsion from the Promised Land, and death). Following the disobedience in the Garden, God showed grace to the first humans by promising the Messiah would mend what had been broken. Genesis 3:15 hints this would involve a sacrificial and atoning death by a specific seed (sg.) from the woman, an element not lost in later translations and interpretations:

MT	LXX	Tg.Ps-J.
וְאֵיבָה ׀ אָשִׁית בֵּינְךָ וּבֵין הָאִשָּׁה וּבֵין זַרְעֲךָ וּבֵין זַרְעָהּ	καὶ ἔχθραν θήσω ἀνὰ μέσον σου καὶ ἀνὰ μέσον τῆς γυναικὸς καὶ ἀνὰ μέσον τοῦ σπέρματός σου καὶ ἀνὰ μέσον τοῦ σπέρματος αὐτῆς	ודבבו אישוי בינך ובין איתתא בין זרעית בנך ובין זרעית בנהא
		ויהי כד יהוון בנהא דאיתתא נטרין מצוותא דאורייתא יהוון מכוונין ומחיין יתך על רישך וכד שבקין מצוותא דאורייתא תהוי
הוּא יְשׁוּפְךָ רֹאשׁ וְאַתָּה תְּשׁוּפֶנּוּ עָקֵב׃	αὐτός σου τηρήσει κεφαλήν καὶ σὺ	מתכווין ונכית יתהון בעיקביהון ברם להון יהי אסו ולך לא יהי אסו ועתידין הינון למיעבד

---

[29] Wilfried Warning, *Literary Artistry in Leviticus*, BibInt 35 (Leiden: Brill, 1999).

[30] Rodríguez, "Leviticus 16: Its Literary Structure," *AUSS* 34.2 (1996): 283.

	τηρήσεις αὐτοῦ πτέρναν	שְׁפִיוּתָא בְּעִיקְבָא בְּיוֹמֵי מַלְכָּא מְשִׁיחָא :
I shall put hostility between you and the woman and between your seed and her seed.	And I will put hostility between you and the woman and between your seed and her seed,	And I will put hostility between you and the woman, and between the seed of your son, and the seed of her sons;
He will crush your head and you will crush his heel.	He shall watch against your head, and you shall watch against his heel.	and it shall be when the sons of the woman keep the commandments of the law, they will be prepared to smite you upon your head; but when they forsake the commandments of the law, you will be ready to bite them in their heel. However, for them there shall be a medicine, but for you there will be no medicine; and they shall make a remedy for the heel in the days of the King Messiah.

This promise is expanded upon throughout the TaNaKh and the sacrificial aspect becomes a focus in the Akedah (Gen 22), Pesach (Exod 12), the yearly feasts (Lev 23), and the sacrificial system (Exod 25 – Lev 17). Davidson notes the eschatological nature of Leviticus 16 and suggests the Day of Atonement is the "eschatological climax of salvation history," he observes "Jewish interpreters" also consider this festival "as representing the day of Judgment"[31]

---

[31] Richard M. Davidson, "The Eschatological Literary Structure of the Old Testament," in *Creation, Life, Hope: Essays in Honor of Jacques B. Doukhan*, ed. Jiří Moskala (Berrien Springs, MI: Old Testament Department, Seventh-day Adventist Theological Seminary, Andrews University, 2000), 360.

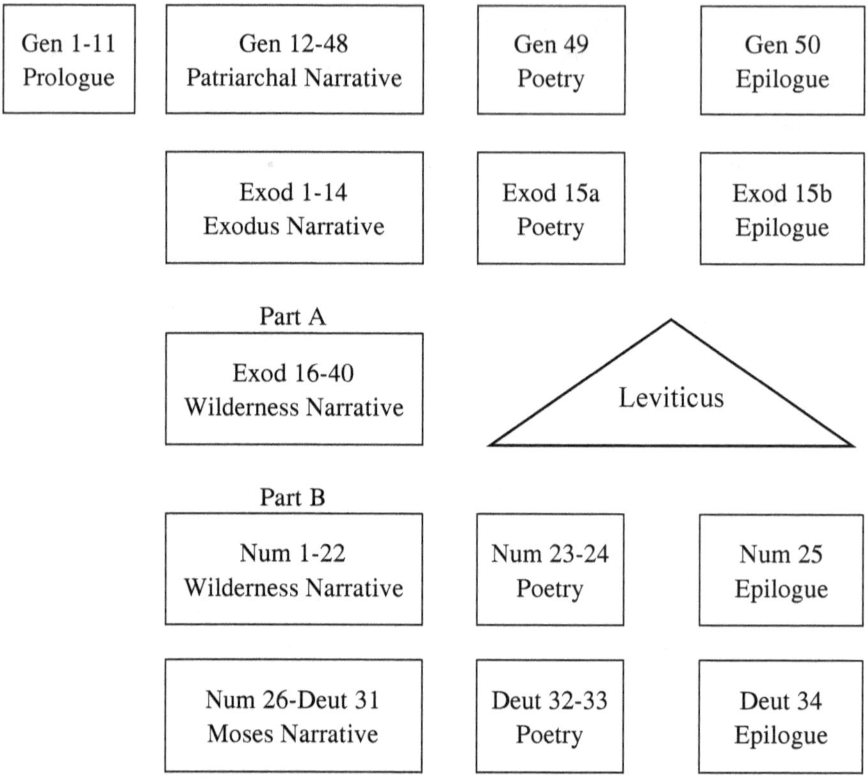

Gen 1-11
Prologue
Gen 12-48
Patriarchal Narrative
Gen 49
Poetry
Gen 50
Epilogue
Exod 1-14
Exodus Narrative
Exod 15a
Poetry
Exod 15b
Epilogue
Part A
Exod 16-40
Wilderness Narrative
Leviticus
Part B
Num 1-22
Wilderness Narrative
Num 23-24
Poetry
Num 25
Epilogue
Num 26-Deut 31
Moses Narrative
Deut 32-33
Poetry
Deut 34
Epilogue
Fig. 6. The four major macro-structural patterns in the Pentateuch.

This structural pattern seems to embrace the whole Pentateuch. The highest level of structure is expressed in Figure 7.

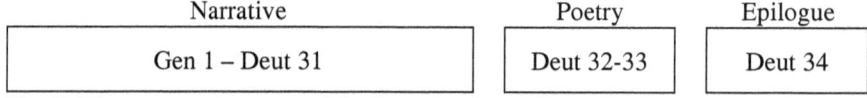

Narrative
Gen 1 – Deut 31
Poetry
Deut 32-33
Epilogue
Deut 34
Fig. 7. The structural pattern of the Pentateuch

"In the Last Days"

From Sailhamer's literary pattern it is possible to find the ultimate purpose of the Pentateuch. In three out of the four macro-structural junctures (Fig. 6), the central character calls together, or addresses, the audience and proclaims, through poetry, what will happen in "the end of days." It is the same Hebrew phrase, באחרית הימים, that is used in all three instances (Gen 49:1, Num 24:14, and Deut 31:29).

This is "a prophetic phrase denoting the final period of the history so far as the speaker's perspective reaches; the sense thus varies with the context, but it often = the ideal or Messianic future."[32] This phrase is only used one other time in the Pentateuch, and that is also within a macro-structural seam (Deut 4:30) The rare use of this phrase makes it an important key to unlock the overall strategy of the author of the Pentateuch.[33]

From this, one can conclude that the purpose of these three major poetic segments was to reveal what would happen with God's people "in the end of days." In other words, the poetic discourses are "eschatological." Sailhamer writes:

> The author shows throughout his work an intense interest in past events. His repeated and strategic return to the notion of "the last days" in giving his work its final shape reveals that his interest is in the future as well.... Because of the terminology he uses (viz., "the end of days"), we could call it an eschatological reading of his historical narratives. The narrative texts of past events are presented as pointers to future events. Past events foreshadow the future.[34]

Sailhamer suggests the purpose of the structure in the Pentateuch may be to demonstrate the relationship between the past and the future. "That which happened to God's people in the past portends of future events. To say it another way, the past is seen as a lesson for the future."[35] Thus, it is important to understand that past events work as pointers to future events, while future events are written to remind the reader of past narratives.[36] He adds the poetic texts both at the micro- and the macro-structural level may suggest "the author wants us to view the stories in the Pentateuch within the context of the prophetic hope in a coming messianic king" ... "suggesting that one of the

---

[32] BDB, 31a. See also, R. Laird Harris, "אָחַר," *TWOT* 1:69 and Andrew E. Hill, "אַחֲרִית," *NIDOTTE* 1:362.

[33] John H. Sailhamer, "The Canonical Approach to the OT: Its Effect on Understanding Prophecy," *JETS* 30 (1987): 310-11.

[34] Sailhamer, *Pentateuch as Narrative*, 37.

[35] Ibid.

[36] For further study on Narrative Typology, see Sailhamer, *Pentateuch as Narrative*, 37-44, and idem, "Canonical Approach to the OT," 307-15.

central issues in the message of the Pentateuch is the coming king and his eternal kingdom."[37] Davidson concurs with Sailhamer and remarks:

> "the author/writer/compiler that brought together the Pentateuch into its final canonical shape had a compositional strategy that cast the entire Pentateuch into an eschatological framework, with the person and work of the coming Messiah at the heart of that eschatological frame. In a sense, then, the Pentateuch as a whole, from beginning to end, may be seen as messianic eschatology."[38]

Davidson notes this eschatological messianic emphasis is also seen in the canonical structure of the TaNaKh, in the stitching connecting the Torah (Ta) and the Prophets (Na) and the stitching connecting the Prophets (Na) and the Writings (Kh). The final redactor of Pentateuch mentions a future prophet who will be a greater than Moses, noting this is still a future event (Deut 34:5-12; Cf. Deut 18:15-16), an intriguing introduction to the Prophetic section of the TaNaKh. The New Testament considers this prophecy fulfilled in the coming of Jesus Christ (Acts 3:18-26; 7:37). A second element emphasized is God's Torah which was given through Moses (Josh 1:1-9). This dual emphasis—an eschatological Messiah and God's Torah is also seen in the stitching connecting the Prophets (Mal 4:1-6 [ET]) and the Writings (Psalm 1 focuses on the Torah and Psalm 2 on the Messiah). The Writings also concludes on these two themes (2 Chr 36; Cf. Is 44:28; 45:1).[39] It is interesting this dual emphasis is also seen in the architectural structure of the Tabernacle which can be divided into two squares (see Fig 8.), the first square has the Altar of Burnt Offering at its center (sacrificial atonement) and the second square has the Ark of the Covenant at its center (God's Torah).

---

[37] Sailhamer, *Meaning of the Pentateuch*, 37.
[38] Davidson, "Eschatological Literary Structure of the Old Testament," 360-61.
[39] For further reading, see ibid., 361-63.

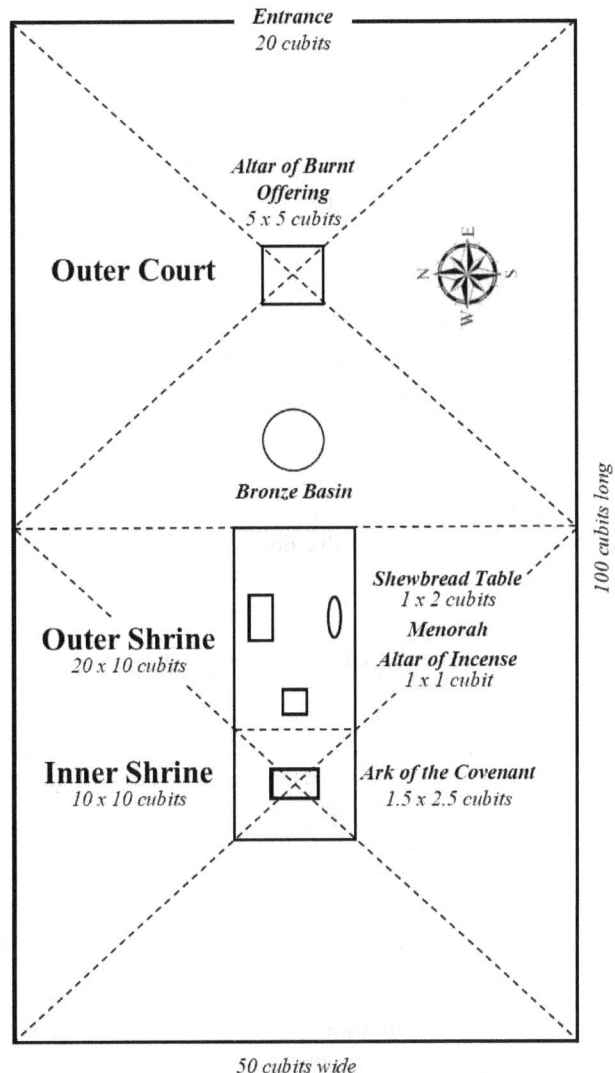

Fig. 8. Floorplan of the Tabernacle. Modified and reconstructed from: Jacob Milgrom, *Leviticus 1-16*, AB 3 (New York: Doubleday, 1991), 135.

Chapter 3 takes a closer look at the poetry in the first major structural pattern of Fig. 6. It explores the eschatological aspect of Jacob's blessing of Joseph.

3. Messianic/Eschatological Implications of the Joseph Oracle

This chapter explores the messianic and eschatological implications of the Joseph oracle in Gen 49 and considers the relationship between Judah and Joseph in light of the promised seed theme, the Abrahamic covenant, and messianic expectations. It concludes by contemplating Joseph as a prophetic type of the coming Messiah.

The Messianic Aspect

The Joseph oracle can be divided into three major parts as shown in Table 9.

Table 9. Three major parts of the Joseph oracle

Section of the Oracle	Verse(s)	Theme
Part 1	v. 22	Joseph compared to a vine or a wild ass
Part 2	vv. 23-24	Joseph's successful self-defense
Part 3	vv. 25-26	Joseph's comprehensive blessing

Nahum M. Sarna has established that:

> There seem to be four themes in the verses directed to Joseph: the attributes of the tribes (v. 22), an historical allusion (vv. 23f.), divine protection (vv. 24f.), and blessings of prosperity (vv. 25f.). This is the only Testament that does not commence with the name of the tribe. This stylistic variance may be intended to draw attention to the special importance of the Joseph tribes.[1]

---

[1] Nahum M. Sarna, *Genesis*, The JPS Torah Commentary (Philadelphia: Jewish Publication Society of America, 1989), 342.

A few comments need to be made before looking into the oracle. As discussed in the previous chapter, Gen 49:22 contains metaphors from the animal world according to some translators, and to the plant world according to others. In either case, Joseph is depicted as a prosperous son, living in an ideal environment, who has everything his heart desires.

This study is not a comprehensive commentary of the oracle, since that would be beyond the scope of the present study, and would be large enough to warrant a study all of its own. Rather, this study will focus on some of the key phrases which are highly pertinent to this topic. The study will examine the Joseph oracle independently from the others, and then it will try to place its findings into the larger contextual picture.

The Suffering Joseph
"With bitterness archers attacked him; they shot at him with hostility" (v. 23).

From portraying Joseph as a prosperous son, Jacob words now became a picture of suffering. Interestingly, the Hebrew word used here for "attacked" is *śātam* (try to do him in). This word occurs only six times in the Old Testament, and three of them involve Jacob in some way (Gen 27:4; 49:23; 50:15). The other three uses are in Job 16:9; 30:21; and Ps 55:4. The verb appears to refer to both feelings of animosity and active hatred. When they heard their father say these words, Joseph's brothers probably understood this as Joseph's persecution under their hands as well as during his years of slavery and imprisonment. Sarna writes,

> Scripture nowhere else records attacks by archers upon Joseph. Unless this refers to some unreported episode in his life or to attacks on Ephraim and Manasseh by neighboring tribes or Canaanite armies, the phraseology may be figurative. It could allude to Ishmaelites,... to the hostility of Joseph's brothers,[2] or to the slanderous accusations of Potiphar's wife with their bitter aftereffects. The figure of slander as an arrow is well attested.[3]

---

[2] This could be supported by the usage of *śātam* in both Gen 49:23 and 50:5. In the last verse, Joseph's brothers fear that Joseph will take revenge now that Jacob has died, and treat them as they had treated him.

[3] Sarna, *Genesis*, 343.

Keil and Kelitzch suggest this verse uses a prophetic perfect verb (the perfect consecutive), describing a future that has already come.[4] From this, the suffering aspects may represent some future events, rather than Joseph's past. This fit well with the above discussion regarding the phrase "in the last days."

It should not be surprising that one finds aspects in the oracle that would draw attention to past events, in this case to Joseph's suffering. At the same time, Joseph's suffering foreshadows and anticipates later events, a future antitypical Joseph. One could expect that God, through the words of Jacob, had this literary technique in mind for the entire oracle.

The Loyal and Protected Joseph

"But his bow remained steady, his strong arms stayed limber ..." (v. 24a).

Victor Hamilton asserts that the enemies of Joseph would not succeed in destroying him because of divine help. God turned back the assault and gave Joseph the strength to defend or fight off his opponents.[5] Gordon Wenham, however, states that "there is no intimation in Genesis of Joseph's agile verbal self-defense against false accusation. Rather, he appears as the sufferer whose appeals go unheeded."[6] It is interesting to note that although it seemed like Joseph's appeals went unheeded, God was still with him. In the larger context, everything turned out to be a blessing. The LXX sees this verse from a different perspective:[7] it considers the bow as the bows of the enemies instead of the bow of Joseph. God destroyed the accusations against Joseph. The LXX reads as follows: "But their bow and arrows were mightily consumed, and the sinews of their arms were slackened by the hand." In the light of the literary technique mentioned above, a future eschatological Joseph would be protected and helped by God in the same way as was the Pentateuchal Joseph. God will be with and protect the person who will stay loyal to Him even during the worst hardships, just like he protected Joseph.

---

[4] C. F. Keil and F. Delitzsch, *The Pentateuch*, trans. James Martin, COT 1 (Edinburgh: T&T Clark, 1872), 406.

[5] Victor P. Hamilton, *The Book of Genesis: Chapters 18-50*, NICOT (Grand Rapids: Eerdmans, 1995), 684.

[6] Wenham, *Genesis 16-50*, 485.

[7] Lancelot C. L. Brenton, *The Septuagint with Apocrypha: Greek and English* (Peabody, MA: Hendrickson, 1995).

The Divine Joseph
> "... *from there is the Shepherd the Stone of Israel.*" (v. 24d)

This phrase in the Joseph oracle seems to carry the strongest element of messianic foreshadowing. The literal translation of the Hebrew text is: "From there [is] a shepherd, the stone of Israel." Derek Kidner contends that this line of the poem "creates an abrupt aside ... for no apparent reason."[8] The stanza would actually be less obscure if this line was left out, so the author must have included this clause for a specific reason. This clause could be understood either as parenthetical or coordinate with the preceding phrase. If parenthetical, the clause could be rendered in three different ways. First, it might suggest that from the time of Joseph's exaltation, he became the shepherd and the stone of Israel. Second, it could imply that from God, the Mighty One of Jacob, Joseph received the strength to become such.[9] In either of these cases, Joseph serves as a type of a coming eschatological Joseph, the good Shepherd, who is the stone, and would be the foundation of Israel. This interpretation would also be in line with Joseph's experience: He indeed became the "shepherd" and savior of his father's house. This notion is further supported by Ps 105:17-23, where the Psalmist states that Joseph was divinely appointed and trained to save his people in time of severe famine. Through him God's redemptive purpose was carried to another step.[10] Joseph became the means of Israel's survival, and would be a type of the coming Messiah. In the third case, this clause could be taken as a messianic prophecy: from Joseph there will come a shepherd, the stone of Israel, the Messiah. The parenthetical view fits perfectly with the Jewish tradition about Messiah son of Joseph, which was considered in chapter 2 above.

If the clause should be understood as coordinate with the preceding phrase, it applies to God Himself. Then the idea expressed is that the hands of Joseph were made strong by the One who is the shepherd and stone of Israel.[11] The parenthetical and the coordinate view do not necessarily have to

---

[8] Derek Kidner, *Genesis: An Introduction and Commentary*, TOTC 1 (Chicago: Inter-Varsity Press, 1967), 221.

[9] Francis D. Nichol, ed., *Genesis to Deuteronomy*, SDABC 1 (Washington, DC: Review & Herald, 1978), 483.

[10] Charles T. Fritsch, "'God Was with Him': A Theological Study of the Joseph Narrative," *Int* 9 (1955): 32.

[11] As pointed out in the translation of this oracle in chapter three, both the term "shepherd" and "stone" have an important meaning in biblical poetry. The "shepherd" is a Divine title on God (Pss 23:1; 80:1; Eccl 12:11) and "stone" is refer-

contradict each other. It would be possible to picture Joseph as a type of the eschatological shepherd and stone of Israel simultaneously to him being made strong by the ultimate shepherd and stone of Israel. This dual interpretation or tension would not be unfamiliar in Eastern thought.[12] Although both views are possible, the parenthetical interpretation is more likely since it is more consistent with the use of the Hebrew word for "from there."

The Blessed Joseph

Jacob's testament to Joseph takes a new shift, this time from suffering to the prosperous promises recorded in verses 25 and 26. Joseph has been a blessing to his father, brothers, the entire clan, to Egypt, and the surrounding nations. And now it is Joseph's turn to be blessed. Jacob assures Joseph that the blessings he bestows on him immeasurably exceeds what he himself received from his forebears. The blessings that Jacob had received (Gen 12:2, 3; 13:16; 18:8f.; 27:29; 28:13-15) did not just include prosperity, but also national and political renown, along with high religious privileges as implied by the "promises."[13] Wenham contends that 'blessing' is one of the keywords of Genesis, occurring some eighty-eight times in the book. In verses 25 and 26 the usage makes an elegant climax. The root occurs six times (verb, 1 time; noun, 5 times), which underlines the notion that "the God-given blessings of the future will far outshine those already experienced."[14]

Wenham also contrasts these blessings with the primeval history, to show that they cover all of the important spheres of human activity.

> Rain from heaven and spring from the deep (cf. 1:2) beneath will ensure fruitful agriculture (contrast 3:17-19), while women will enjoy the blessing of many children (contrast 3:16). In the Hebrew there is alliteration between "heaven" (שמים - šāmayim) and "breast" (שד - šādayim), "deep" (תהות - tĕhôm) and "womb" (רחם - rehem). This deliberate balanc-

---

ring to the coming Messiah (Isa 8:14; 28:16). See the above translation on this line of the poem.

[12] For further study on Jewish thought, see for instance Doukhan, *Drinking at the Sources,* 191-218, and Marvin R. Wilson, *Our Father Abraham* (Grand Rapids: Eerdmans, 1989), 154-56.

[13] S. R. Driver, *The Book of Genesis*, 14th ed. (London: Methuen & Co., 1943), 393.

[14] Wenham, *Genesis 16-50,* 486.

ing of divine blessing on male and female spheres of interest suggests the completeness of God's promises to all Joseph's descendants, both men and women.[15]

All these blessings were to rest on the head of Joseph, on the brow of the *nāzīr*, of his brothers.

The Royal Joseph
"... *on the crown of the prince among his brothers.*" (v. 26d)
The concluding clause of this oracle has a royal flavor. The key word used is the noun נָזִיר, which could be translated as one who is consecrated or set apart.[16] One could be set apart by rank or by specific vows of abstinence (Num 6:2; Judg 13:5; Amos 2:1), in a religious sense. The verb נָזַר means dedicated or consecrated. The noun נֵזֶר means consecration, crown, Naziriteship (Num 6:4, 5, 7, 8, 12, 13), or could even refer to the "diadem," which a king or a priest would (Exod 29:6; 39:30; Lev 8:9; 2 Sam 1:10; 2 Kgs 11:12; Pss 89:40; 132:18) wear as a sign of his royal power and/or consecration.[17]

From this, the last clause could then carry several meanings. First, Joseph was "separated from" his brothers, and thus marked out for special distinction and service. Second, he was distinguished because of his high rank, something conferred on him by his father. "He who was once separated from his brothers through spite is now separated from his brothers by blessing."[18] Third, it could describe Joseph as a "prince" and imply a coming kingship of the Joseph tribe. All three interpretations of *nāzīr* make perfect sense. Joseph did a special service for his family. He did receive a special blessing from his father. And the sum of his fathers' blessings would indicate rulership.[19]

The third meaning might be supported by the parallel text in Deut 33:13-17, which was pronounced by Moses just before his death. In this passage the same word, *nāzīr*, is used to describe Joseph, but in this oracle an explanation has been added. It describes Joseph as a king who would not on-

---

[15] Ibid., 486-87.
[16] BDB, 634c.
[17] Hamilton, *Book of Genesis: Chapters 18-50*, 683, and BDB, 634b.
[18] Hamilton, *Book of Genesis: Chapters 18-50*, 686.
[19] For a further study on patriarchal rulership, see B. J. van der Merwe, "Joseph as Successor of Jacob," in *Studia Biblica et Semitica*, ed. Theodoro Christiano Vriezen (Wageningen, Nederlands: H. Veenman, 1966), 221-32.

ly rule over his brothers, but have power and influence over the entire world.[20] If this passage really presupposes the royalty and leadership of Joseph and his tribe, are there any indications of this in history?

Many of Israel's leaders were from Joseph's (Ephraim/Manasseh) tribe. Joshua, for instance, who took over the leadership after Moses and led God's people into the promised land, was a descendant of Joseph. About a third of the land of Canaan was possessed by the two tribes of Joseph.[21] Figure 8 shows the boundaries of the land areas distributed to the twelve tribes after Joshua's conquest of Canaan.

Three out of the twelve named judges in the book of Judges were from the tribes of Joseph. They were Deborah, Gideon, and Abdon.[22] Samuel, the last judge and leader before the kingdom period, was also from a Joseph tribe. Table 10 lists the judges who ruled in Israel between 1406 BCE and 1385 BCE. The highlighted king and judges were from "the tribe of Joseph."

Interestingly, when the Davidic Kingdom was divided into two parts, the northern and the southern kingdoms, due to the economic policies of King Solomon and his successor Rehoboam, one tribe remained under the Davidic rulership of Rehoboam whereas the ten northern tribes of Israel were led by Jeroboam from the tribe of Ephraim. After the division, Ephraim and Judah represented God's people.

---

[20] The Hebrew word used here for power over the nations is נגח which means push, thrust, or gore (see BDB, 618c). The same root word is used in 1 Kgs 22:11; 2 Chr 18:10; Dan 8:4. Although the world is used in connection with extending the boundaries of the land, either by war or crushing the enemy, the purpose is to control and rule over the area. This was God's plan when they entered Canaan, but it was also His long-term plan that His kingdom would fill up the entire world (Gen 12:1-3; Exod 19:6).

[21] Although they were the largest tribes, comprised of 14 percent of the total number of Israelites (85,200 men from the tribe of Manasseh and Ephraim /624,730 total men of Israel, according to Num 26), this is not in proportion to the land mass they were given.

[22] It is mentioned in Judg 9 that Abimelech, from the tribe of Manasseh, was elected king over Israel. Although he did not rule for more than three years and he only ruled over a limited area (Shechem and the surrounding area), this was the first experiment with Israelite kingship.

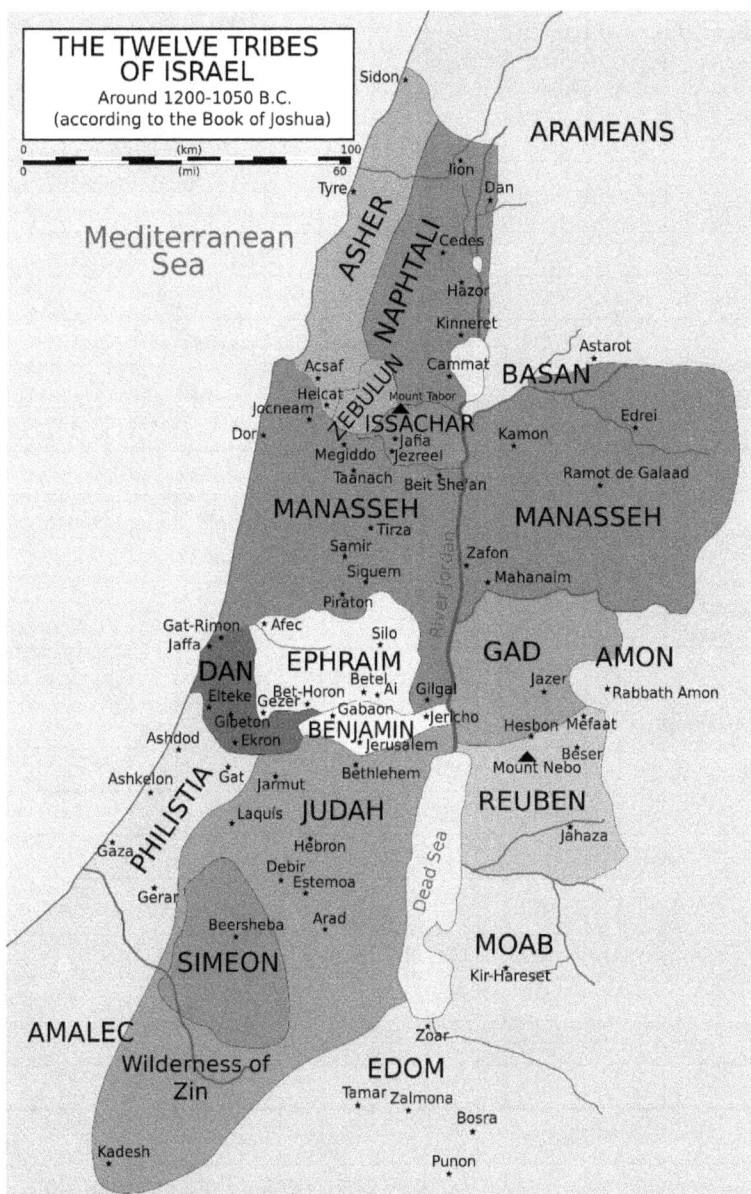

Fig. 9. Map of Canaan and the territories of the twelve tribes of Israel according to the Book of Joshua. *Source*: https://commons.wikimedia.org/wiki/ File%3A12_Tribes_of_Israel_Map.svg.
Attribution: By 12 tribus de Israel.svg: Translated by Kordas 12 staemme israels heb.svg: by user:יוסי 12 staemme israels.png: by user:Janz derivative work: Richardprins [CC-BY-SA-3.0 (http://creativecommons.org/licenses/by-sa/3.0/) or GFDL (http://www.gnu.org/copyleft/fdl.html)], via Wikimedia Commons

Table 10. Chronology of the Judges

Oppressor	King	YEARS	Estimated Dates BCE	Ref. (Judges)	Judge	Tribe	YEARS	Place of Battle
Mesopotamia	Cushan-rishathaim	8	1385-1377	3:8				
			1377-1337	3:9-11	Othniel	Judah	40	
Moabites	Eglon	18		3:12-14				
			1319-1239	3:15-30	Ehud	Benjamin	80	Jericho
Philistines				3:31				
			1337-1319	3:31	Shamgar			
Canaanites	Jabin	20	1259-1239	4:2-3				
			1239-1199	4:4-5:31	Deborah	Ephraim	40	Esdraelon
Midianites	Oreb, Zeeb, Zebah, Zalmunna	7	1199-1192	6:1-6				
			1192-1152	6:7-8:35	Gideon	Manasseh	40	Hill of Moreh
Civil war of Abimelech			1152-1149	9	Killed at Thebez			
			1149-1126	10:1-2	Tola	Issachar	23	
			1126-1104	10:3-6	Jair	Gilead	22	
Ammonites		18	1104-1086	10:7-9				
			1086-1080	10:10-12:7	Jephthah	Gilead	6	Transjordan
			1080-1072	12:8-10	Ibzan	Judah	8	
			1072-1062	12:11-12	Elon	Zebulun	10	
			1062-1055	12:13-15	Abdon	Ephraim	7	
Philistines		40	1115-1075	13:1				
			1075-1055	13:2-16:31	Samson	Dan	20	

Source: Walton, *Chronological and Background Charts of the Old Testament*, 26.

Although the Joseph tribes were in ruling positions during certain periods after the oracles were given, they were far from rulers over the whole world. If one notes the messianic undertones in the Joseph oracles, this unfulfilled prophecy would be fulfilled by the eschatological Joseph, the promised seed, the coming Messiah who will rule all the nations (Fig. 10 shows the

Genealogies of the Messiah ben Joseph, Messiah ben Levi, and Messiah ben David).

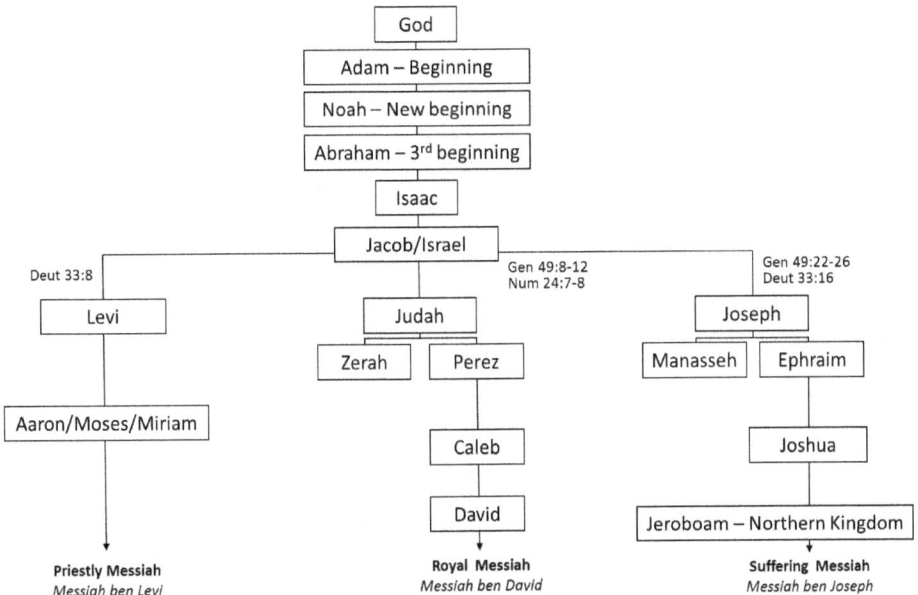

Fig. 10. The genealogies of Messiah ben Joseph, Messiah ben Levi, and Messiah ben David.

At this point, some contradictions become apparent. According to the Judah oracle (Gen 49:8-11), Judah will have leadership over the nations and among his brothers. The promised seed will come from the line of Judah. In addition, it seems like Judah receives the blessings normally associated with the birthright. Therefore, who is the rightful heir of Jacob and the Abrahamic promises?

The Relationship between Judah and Joseph

A key passage in Genesis is the divine Announcement of 12:1-3. Laurence Turner observes it is either directly related to or may be brought into connection with everything that follows.[23] Thus, the two questions in the remaining part of the Scripture are: "Who would be the new heir of these

---

[23] Laurence A. Turner, *Announcements of Plot in Genesis*, JSOTSupp 96 (Sheffield: Sheffield Academic Press, 1990), 51.

promises and give birth to the seed?" and "How or when will these promises be fulfilled?" The Announcement consists of the following promises:

1. I will make of you a great nation — 12:2a
2. I will bless you — 12:2b
3. I will make your name great — 12:2c
4. You will be a blessing — 12:2d
5. I will bless those who bless you — 12:3a
6. I will curse the one who curses you — 12:3b
7. Everyone will be blessed through you — 12:3c

The Blessings of Judah, Joseph, and the Patriarchs Compared

When comparing these seven blessings with the oracle of Joseph and Judah, one notices some striking similarities. The two oracles can be outlined as shown in Table 11.

Table 11. Comparison between the Joseph and Judah oracles

Themes	Joseph		Judah	
	Gen 49:22-26	Deut 33:13-17	Gen 49:8-12	Deut 33:7
Prosperous	22			
Suffering	23			
Protected	24-25			7
Messianic	24c		10-12	
Blessed	25b-26	13-16	11-12	
Leadership	26d	16c	8	
Great Nation		17	10	

Although both Judah and Joseph were blessed through the oracle, there is one major difference. In Judah's case, the blessings are bestowed on the Shiloh, who is spoken of in verse 10.[24] On the other hand, the blessings were to rest on Joseph's head (his tribes). It is in fact stated that the blessing given to Joseph would be greater than his forefathers'. One should also note the similarities in the language used in the blessing given to Jacob (Gen

---

[24] J. Blenkinsopp, "The Oracle of Judah and the Messianic Entry," *JBL* 80 (1961): 60.

27:27-29) and the Joseph blessing (Gen 49:22-26; Deut 33:13-17). This in itself could lead one to the conclusion that Joseph, rather than Judah, was the successor of Jacob.

Joseph, the Rightful Heir

Van der Merwe[25] notes that Jacob's "blessings" in Gen 49:1-27 come at a very crucial point. They interrupt the deathbed narrative just when Jacob has entrusted Shechem[26] to Joseph (48:22), which would be strange if Judah was the heir. It is also interesting that Jacob does not refer to the birthright in the narrative, but merely mentions it in the account of how Ephraim was preferred above Manasseh when they were adopted (48:5, 13-20) and in the poem (49:3, 4). This is significant when considering what an important role this issue played in the Abraham and Isaac narrative. In 1 Chr 5:1, it is stated that the birthright was given to Joseph's sons and in verse 2 it is explicitly stated that Joseph received the birthright. This passage is important as it confirms that it was Joseph who received the birthright. It also glorifies the tribes of Joseph at the expense of Judah even in the Second Temple period, which was after the deportation of Israel by the Assyrian army. From this, it is seen that the biblical writer understood that Joseph received the double portion which belonged to the firstborn when Joseph's two sons were adopted by Jacob.

Deuteronomy 21:15-17, which deals with the right of the firstborn, seems to be patterned after Jacob's marriage and deathbed wishes. It is written from a standpoint that assumes Joseph was given the birthright. Joseph was the son of the beloved wife of Jacob and he was given the rights of the firstborn (the double share of all Jacob's possessions).

Van der Merwe also draws attention to the strong resemblance between Gen 47:29 and 1 Kgs 2:1.

> In the latter text king David on his deathbed called and instructed his successor, Solomon. In the hour of his death Jacob called Joseph. The implication is clear: Jacob called the son he appointed as successor, i.e. Joseph and not Judah.[27]

---

[25] Van der Merwe, "Joseph as Successor of Jacob," 221-32.

[26] This city later became the royal residence of Jeroboam, in northern Israel (1 Kgs 12:25).

[27] Van der Merwe, "Joseph as Successor of Jacob," 225.

There seems to be a trace of narrative in Genesis 48 about the blessing by Jacob of Joseph as a firstborn, in between the blessing of Ephraim and Manasseh. This narrative might be seen in Gen 48:2-4, 7, 15, 16a, 21f. A blessing of Joseph is explicitly mentioned in v. 15, and it culminates in giving Shechem to Joseph.

The fact that Jacob adopted Manasseh and Ephraim and let them have an equal share in the division of the inheritance strengthens the idea that Joseph succeeded Jacob. "This adoption of Ephraim and Manasseh by Jacob was equivalent to giving Joseph the double portion of the inheritance, i.e. the equivalent of the inheritance to which the first-born was entitled."[28] Joseph's two sons were not only adopted by Jacob, but they were established as the legitimate continuation of the patriarch's generation.

It is interesting to note the importance that barrenness plays in the Genesis narrative. The Scripture mentions that Sarah, Rebekah, and Rachel were all barren (Gen 11:30; 25:21; 29:3). When a barren woman in the Bible conceived, with God's help, she gave birth to a male child who would be of special importance in the continuing narrative. Sarai gave birth to Isaac, Rebekah to Esau and Jacob, and Rachel to Joseph.[29] One also notices that it is often the firstborn son of the "barren" woman who receives the birthright with its blessings. Thus, the fact that the firstborn son of the patriarchs in the Genesis narrative never received the blessing of the firstborn that belonged to him[30] the conclusion is supported that Joseph was Jacob's heir.

Regarding the lifespan of the different patriarchs, Stanley Gevirtz and James Williams make an interesting, but quite possibly coincidental, observation. They note that the age of the patriarchs could be factored as shown in Table 12. Gevirtz suggests that the ages of the three first patriarchs "are formed as multiples of square numbers that constitute a succession,"[31] and that Joseph's life span is the sum of this sequence of consecutive square

---

[28] Ibid., 226; see Deut 21:15-17 and 1 Chr 5:1.

[29] In addition to women in Genesis, Manoah's wife (Judg 13:2), Hannah (1 Sam 1:5), and Elizabeth (Luke 1:7) were also barren. They gave birth to Samson, Samuel, and John the Baptist respectively.

[30] This explains why Esau did not receive the birthright, although Rebekah had been barren. For further study, see Roger Syren, *The Forsaken First-Born: A Study of a Recurrent Motif in the Patriarchal Narratives*, JSOTSupp 133 (Sheffield: JSOT Press, 1993).

[31] Stanley Gevirtz, "The Life Spans of Joseph and Enoch and the Parallelism šib'ātayim — šib'îm wěšib'āb," *JBL* 96 (1977): 571.

numbers.[32] James Williams takes the numerical pattern one step further and asserts that "Joseph is the *successor* in the pattern (7→5→3→1) and the *sum* of his predecessors ($5^2+6^2+7^2$)."[33] More evidence is needed to substantiate if this is intentional by the writers, and, if indeed, biblical writers and redactors were partial to this type of mathematics. Regardless, Williams implies that Joseph may be the next heir of the promises based on this observation.

Judging from the reaction of Joseph's brothers and father when hearing about his dreams (Gen 37:5-8, 10), there is no doubt that they understood their meaning: Joseph would rule over them and the clan.

Table 12. The age of the patriarchs

Name	Age when died	Reference	Factors
Abraham	175	Gen 25:7	$7 \times 5^2 = 175$
Isaac	180	Gen 35:28-29	$5 \times 6^2 = 180$
Jacob	147	Gen 47:28	$3 \times 7^2 = 147$
Joseph	110	Gen 50:22	$1 \times (5^2 + 6^2 + 7^2) = 110$

From the preceding discussion, one can conclude that Joseph was the appointed first-born of Jacob who, consequently, became the successor of Jacob as ruler of the "clan,"[34] and was singled out to receive his father's blessings and to be a blessing.[35] It is important to note that the poem in Gen

---

[32] Ibid.

[33] James G. Williams, "Number Symbolism and Joseph as a Symbol of Completion," *JBL* 98 (1979): 86-87.

[34] This point could be supported by the following evidence mentioned by Van der Merwe, "Joseph as Successor of Jacob," passim. First, Joseph made all the arrangements in connection with the funeral. Second, in Genesis 50 Joseph actually steps into the place of his father or parallels him (Gen 47:27 vs. 50:22; 47:28 vs. 50:22, 26; 48:5, 12 vs. 50:23). Both Joseph and Jacob had the same type of funeral (50:2, 3 vs. 50:26), and both predicted the Exodus (48:21 vs. 50:25). Joseph's brothers accepted Joseph's supremacy (50:18, 21).

[35] T. Desmond Alexander, "Messianic Ideology in the Book of Genesis," in *The Lord's Anointed: Interpretation of Old Testament Messianic Texts*, ed. Philip E. Satterthwaite, Richard S. Hess, and Gordon J. Wenham (Grand Rapids: Baker, 1995), 26.

49:1-27 attributes to Judah something which is always assigned to Joseph in the surrounding narrative, and that is the phrase "your fathers' sons will bow down to you." These words imply the supremacy of Judah. One should not overlook the possibility that in the future the descendants of both Judah and Joseph, at different points or at the same time in history, did experience supremacy over the other brothers. There is little doubt, however, that Joseph had the role of leadership after Jacob's death (Gen 37:7, 9; 42:6; 43:26; 44:14; 50:18).

What About the Seed?

Desmond Alexander suggests there are two keywords in Genesis, the first is תּוֹלְדוֹת, g*enerations*, and the second is זֶרַע, *seed*. The word "seed" may denote either a single seed or many seeds. It also implies a close resemblance between progenitor and progeny. "These two terms together focus attention on a unique image which begins with Adam and concludes with the sons of Israel. This family line forms 'the backbone of the book'."[36]

This line is traced through male descendants and the successive member is always clearly identified. The line goes as follows: Adam → Seth → Noah → Shem → Terah → Abraham → Isaac → Jacob → Joseph. This line is dependent upon God; the members of the line often resemble each other; it is often associated with the divine promises; and lastly, there are strong indications that in some way the main line of descent in Genesis is viewed as anticipating a royal line, based on Gen 3:15. In light of this, the "seed" will eventually become a royal dynasty.

When reading the testament of Jacob, one soon discovers that the oracle to Judah is about the coming monarch, the coming seed promised to Adam and Eve. This is much more messianic than the oracle to Joseph, which just has a messianic flavor. This is further supported by the attention showed to and the language used to describe Judah's descendants (Gen 38:9, 27-30). How can both Judah and Joseph be the "seed" of Jacob? Were the promises divided between them so that some fell on Joseph and others on Judah?

While it is outside of the scope of this study to explore these questions thoroughly, the answers might lie in the change of emphasis in the Abrahamic promises. Abraham and Isaac's sons each represented the forefather of a coming people or nation. With this in mind, one can understand why it was so important who should receive the promises, which nation would be

---

[36] Alexander, "From Adam to Judah," 22-23.

blessed, grow strong, and have Messiah among them. In Jacob's case it was different. All of his sons would be part of the Israelite nation. Each son would represent one tribe. The Abrahamic blessing would, in general, be for all of them, although certain aspects of the blessings would fall only on selected tribes—in this case, on Joseph and Judah. When comparing the two oracles of Joseph and Judah, one discovers that Joseph's oracle primarily focuses on blessing and suffering whereas Judah's was on the coming kingship (although they each carry an undertone of the other's primary focus).

Jacques Doukhan suggests there was an important Jewish tradition where the coming Messiah would be both a victim and a priest. This duality can be found in Gen 3:15. Doukhan writes:

> The person meant by the "posterity of the woman" was to be at the same time the priest who bruised evil and made expiation for it, and the victim who would die doing it. This double messianic function explains the reason why the Messiah speaks of His identity in terms of two faces.[37]

A third face of the coming Messiah is that of a majestic king, who was predestined for glory and will rule for eternity. From these comes: Messiah ben Joseph, Messiah ben Levi, and Messiah ben David (Judah). Doukhan states further that the Messiah is designated as a son of Joseph when he is the victim, and as the son of David when He is the king. It is important that suffering and death were not the only destiny of the son of Joseph, but Messiah ben Joseph also appears with the bearing of a glorious Messiah. At the same time, the Talmud speaks expressly of the death of the son of David. Even the suffering Messiah in Isaiah 53 is identified as the Messiah king, Messiah son of David.

From this, the three Messiahs could be seen as one. Doukhan concludes that "the discussion of the rabbis seem only to try to understand the composite figure of the Messiah, for the various names they give Him are aimed, rather, at disclosing some aspect of His personality."[38]

---

[37] Doukhan, *Drinking at the Sources*, 51.

[38] Ibid., 52. For further study, see Doukhan, *Drinking at the Sources*, 44-57, and Heineman, "Messiah of Ephraim," 339-52, and Liver, "Doctrine of the Two Messiahs," 354-90.

The Eschatological Aspect

The Joseph oracle seems to have some very strong messianic aspects. However, before one can draw a messianic application from them, a decision must be made about whether they are prophetic, typological, or just an illustration.

Joseph as an Illustration, Type, or Prophecy?

Reaching a conclusion regarding the three concepts of illustration, type, and prophecy may be complicated because they overlap each other. This is outside of the scope of this study, and is best suited to an individual study given its complexity. However, a few general observations may lead to a preliminary hypothesis. Normally, a prophecy and an illustration do not overlap, that is, a prophecy cannot also be an illustration and vice versa. Only a type combines these two aspects. A type is inherently both a prophecy and an illustration.

With this definition in mind, it could be concluded that the Joseph oracle, or Joseph himself, is not only an illustration, but a true prophetic type. This harmonizes with Sailhamer's theory on narrative typology referred to earlier. Richard Davidson defines typology within the Christian context as "a study of the Old Testament salvation historical realities or 'types' (persons, events, institutions) which God has specifically designed to correspond to, and predictively prefigure, their intensified antitypical fulfillment aspects (inaugurated, appropriated, consummated) in New Testament salvation history."[39] This definition could be easily amended to also include a Jewish context by changing the latter half of the definition pertaining to New Testament salvation history to: antitypical eschatological fulfillment in the Messiah as the eschaton is yet to come.

Davidson continues by pointing out five distinguishing characteristics of typology—the Historical, Eschatological, Christological-Soteriological, Ecclesiological, and Prophetic elements. Table 13 by Davidson explains these five basic elements in more details:[40]

---

[39] Richard M. Davidson, "The Eschatological Hermeneutic of Biblical Typology," *TheoRhēma* 6.2 (2011): 12.

[40] Ibid., 11-12.

TABLE 13. Basic elements of biblical typology – Richard M. Davidson

1.	The **historical element** underscores the fact that typology is rooted in history. Three crucial aspects are involved: (1) both type and antitype are *historical realities* (persons, events, institutions) whose historicity is assumed and essential to the typological argument; (2) there is an *historical correspondence* between type and antitype which moves beyond general parallel situations to specific corresponding details; (3) there is an *escalation* or *intensification* from the type to antitype.
2.	The **eschatological ("end-time") element** of typology further clarifies the nature of the historical correspondence and intensification between type and antitype. The Old Testament realities are not just linked to any similar realities, but to their eschatological fulfillment. Three possible aspects of the eschatological fulfillment may be in view: (1) *"inaugurated,"* connected with the first Advent of Christ; (2) *"appropriated,"* focusing on the time of the Church living in tension between the "already" and the "not yet"; and (3) *"consummated,"* linked to the Apocalyptic Second Coming of Christ.
3.	The **Christological (Christ-centered)-soteriological (salvation-centered) element** of biblical typology points out its essential focus and thrust. The Old Testament types are not merely "bare" realities, but *salvific realities*, and find their fulfillment in the person and work of Christ and/or gospel realities brought about by Christ. Christ is thus the ultimate orientation point of Old Testament types and their New Testament fulfillments.
4.	The **ecclesiological (church-related) element** of biblical typology points to three possible aspects of the Church that may be involved in the typological fulfillment: the *individual worshipers*, the *corporate community*, and/or the *sacraments* (baptism and Lord's Supper).
5.	The **prophetic element** of biblical typology involves three essential points. First, the Old Testament type is an *advance-presentation* or prefiguration of the corresponding New Testament antitype. Second, the type is *divinely designed* to prefigure the New Testament antitype. And third, there is a *"must-needs-be"* quality about the Old Testament type, giving it the force of a prophetic/predictive foreshadowing of the New Testament fulfillment.

Typological Indicator

Since it is not explicitly mentioned that Joseph is a type of the Messiah, one has to look for indicators accompanying the Joseph narrative or that come sometime before the appearance of the antitype. The typological indicator in the Joseph narrative is the Joseph oracle. As mentioned earlier, the oracle reveals what will happen in the future. It takes different aspects of Joseph's life and declares that one could expect a future character who will go through these same experiences. Table 14 shows the type, indicator, and the antitype.

Table 14. Joseph as a type

Old Testament Type	**Old Testament Indicator**	Antitype
Joseph Gen 37-50	**Joseph Oracle** **Gen 49:22-26**	Antitypical Joseph The Messiah

The typological indicator draws aspects from the Joseph narrative and points them forward to the antitypical Joseph, the coming Messiah. Thus, within a Jewish context the antitypical fulfillment would be realized in the coming of the Messiah ben Joseph in the eschatological age. In a Christian context, it is believed that Jesus was the antitypical fulfillment. Table 15 lists aspects of Joseph's life which the Joseph oracle alludes to and shows how these aspects were fulfilled in the life of Jesus Christ.

From this table, it becomes clear that Joseph fulfills all the typological characteristics articulated by Davidson. Therefore, it could be concluded that Christian believers have an exegetical foundation to consider Joseph as a type for Jesus Christ—who, like Joseph suffered, saved the world, was a blessing, and offered salvation to anyone who would accept it.

Having established, within the Christian context that Joseph could function as a type for Jesus, one could start to draw parallels between Joseph's life and that of Jesus. Since there are so many similarities, in the interest of brevity, the next section will focus on only a few.[41]

---

[41] For a more elaborate list of similarities, see Patrick Fairbairn, *Typology of Scripture*, 2 vols. (Grand Rapids: Kregel, 1989), and Andrew Jukes, *Types in Genesis* (Grand Rapids: Kregel, 1976).

Table 15. Typological aspect in the Joseph oracle

Joseph Narrative		Joseph Oracle		Anti-typical Joseph
The favored son	37:2-11	Prosperous Tree	v. 22	John 1:1-3; 3:16
Brothers Potiphar's wife	37:12-36 39:19-40:23	Suffering	v.23	Isa 53; Matt 26-27; Mark 9:12c
God was with him Joseph was loyal	39:2-4, 21-23 39:9; 40:8; 41:16	Protected/ Loyal	vv. 24-25	Matt 4:11; 26:45, 53; Luke 22:53 Matt 26:39-46; Luke 22:42-44
Sent by God	45:5-8	Divine	v.24c	Matt 25:54; John 3:16-17; Rom 5:18-19
Blessed Blessing Children	39:4-6, 21-26 41:41-49 41:50-52	Blessed	vv. 24b-26	Mark 14:16b-62 John 3:16-17; Rev 5:12-13 Rev 14
Placed in charge	41:41-44; 48:22	Royal	v. 26d	Matt 16:27; 24:30; 26:64 Luke 20:41-44; Rev 1:5-6
Increase in number	48:15-16	Great Nation	Deut 33:17	Rev 11:15; 19:6, 16

Jesus, the Antitypical Joseph
Structure of the Joseph Narrative

As shown in Figure 11, Errol McGuire has devised the following pattern of movement in the Joseph narrative. It starts with a high point when Joseph is with his father. It then proceeds down into the period of suffering (pit – servanthood – prison), and then finally back up to a second pinnacle. The twin peaks represent Joseph's loving relationship with his father, presumably at home, while the low points express Joseph's trials—when he is separated from his father and home.[42] The Joseph oracle has been structured in the same way, except it does not have the double low points. This might be explained by the fact that the oracle has summarized Joseph's life, looking at

---

[42] Errol McGuire, "The Joseph Story: A Tale of Son and Father," in *Images of Man and God: Old Testament Short Stories in Literary Focus*, ed. Burke O. Long (Sheffield: Almond Press, 1981), 24-25.

the suffering period as one interval. See Figure 12. Not too surprisingly, one could make a similar structure from Jesus' life based on Phil 2:6-12, see Figure 13.

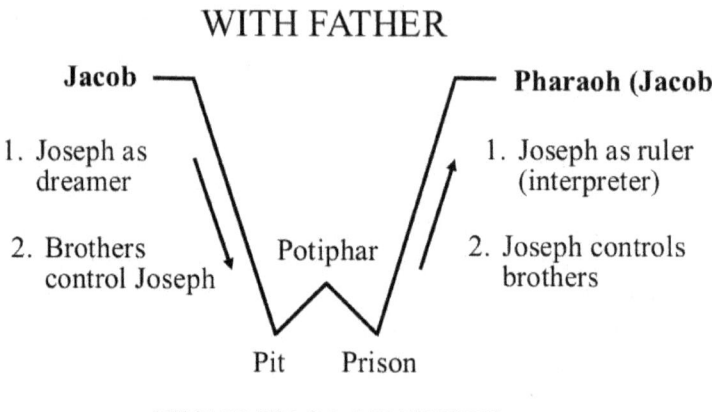

Fig. 11. The Joseph narrative. Modified and reconstructed from: McGuire, "The Joseph Story," 24.

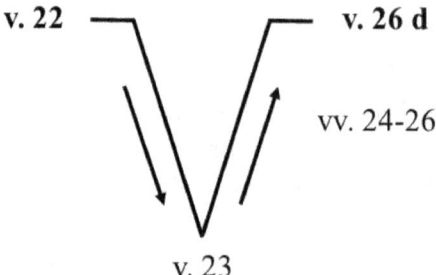

Fig. 12. The Joseph oracle.

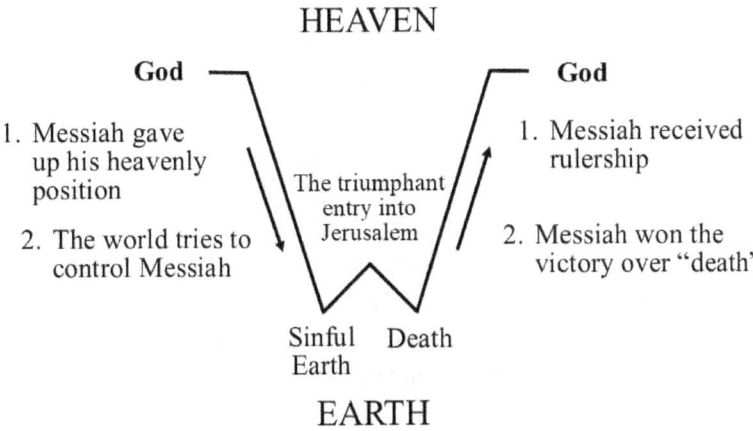

Fig. 13. An outline of Jesus' life.

Joseph's Dreams

A different element pointing forward to the Messiah is Joseph's second dream. Both of the dreams predicted Joseph's coming supremacy. According to Turner, only the first dream was ever fulfilled.[43] The second dream required supremacy not only over his brothers, but also over his father and mother. This element in itself made the second dream impossible to fulfill since Joseph's mother had passed away long before he had the dream. There is no mention of Jacob bowing down to Joseph either, but the narrative does mention that Joseph bowed down to Jacob (Gen 48:12). This theme is repeated in the oracles in Gen 49:22-26 and Deut 33:13-17, where the rulership aspect will encompass the whole earth—an element which was never completely fulfilled. Thus, this prophecy must point forward to a future person. From Rev 11:15; 12:5; 19:16 Christians can surmise that Joseph's dream and oracles were pointing forward to the antitypical Joseph, Jesus Christ, who would rule universally.

---

[43] See Turner's discussion in *Announcements of Plot in Genesis*, 143-83.

Be a Blessing

One of the promises given to Abraham in Gen 12:1-3 was: "All peoples on earth will be blessed through you." In the continuation of the narrative it becomes apparent that Abraham personally provided limited blessings to the world. His most heroic act was to save his nephew from the five kings and intercede for Lot's life when Sodom and Gomorrah were about to be destroyed. In both cases Abraham may have acted for selfish reasons, particularly if he regarded Lot as a potential heir who would fulfill God's promises. No readily identifiable blessings are associated with Isaac either. Rather, he was just a minor character in a narrative where his wife Rebekah took center stage. Jacob also had his ups and downs, but did not turn out to be a blessing, in the contextual sense of the word.

Joseph, however, was a blessing. Not only did he save God's chosen people from death, but also anyone else who was interested in receiving help. In Gen 41:57, it is written that "all the countries came to Egypt to buy grain from Joseph, because the famine was severe in all the world." The same chapter tells that Pharaoh gave Joseph the name "Zaphenath-Paneah" (Gen 41:45) which, Alfred Jones claims, has the possible meaning of "Savior of the age."[44] When looking at Joseph, it appears the promise was fulfilled; however, Joseph was only a type of the coming Messiah. The antitypical Messiah would be the ultimate savior and blessing.

Forgiver

> No one can read about the cruelty of Joseph's brethren without becoming incensed at them. The actions of Potiphar's wife makes us loathe her. Our heart goes out for Joseph as he languishes in prison for a crime he never committed.[45]

The foremost question in the reader's mind, when reading the Joseph narrative, is what will Joseph do when he has his chance to take revenge? With all the hardship he has gone through, one would expect Joseph to give his brothers and Potiphar's wife a well-deserved punishment. Instead, Joseph forgave

---

[44] Alfred Jones, "Zaphnath-Paaneah," *Jones' Dictionary of Old Testament Proper Names*, 369.

[45] Fritsch, "'God Was with Him'," 22.

his brothers, but not only that, he also provided them with all the food they needed and desirable land in Egypt.

For Christians, this aspect of Joseph also foreshadows the ultimate Forgiver. Instead of giving the world its well-deserved punishment, Jesus took the penalty on himself and forgave Earth's inhabitants (Rom 5:8). Additionally, he provides his people with all the spiritual food they needed, and promised them a New Earth (Rev 21-22).

The Separated One

Thomas Whitelaw presents five ways that Joseph was separate from his brothers. Similarly, the eschatological Joseph—Messiah—will also be separate, but in a much greater sense. Joseph was separated from his brothers in the following five ways, and for Christians who have the luxury of the antitypical Joseph having already appeared, making comparisons between Joseph and Jesus becomes easier than for Jews who are still awaiting the eschatological Joseph. Whitelaw proposes the following illustrations:

1. *In his father's love.* Joseph was Jacob's favorite son and was loved more than any of his brothers. Jesus also was the unique and loved son of the Father (Gen 37:3; John 3:16).

2. *In his morality.* Joseph did not take part in his brothers' evil. Jesus was also found without sin (Gen 37:2; Heb 4:15).

3. *In his communication with God.* Joseph was made the receiver of dreams and keeper of Divine secrets. Jesus was also filled with God's spirit and knew His Father's will (Gen 37:5-11; 40:12-22; 41:16-2; John 1:14).

4. *In his suffering.* "Joseph was hated, sold, and practically given over to death by his brothers." Jesus was also hated and rejected by His "brothers," and took mankind's suffering and death (Isa 53).

5. *In his future glory.* Joseph became the second in command of Egypt and the savior of all people. Jesus was also exalted to be Prince, and a savior for humankind (Gen 41:41-44, 56; and Rev 11:15).[46]

The Threefold Eschatological Aspect

Davidson proposes that, for Christians, all types have three aspects of the one eschatological fulfillment of the Old Testament types (see Appendix 2) – the inaugurated aspect which relates to the first Advent; the appro-

---

[46] Thomas Whitelaw, *Genesis and Exodus*, Pulpit Commentary 1 (Grand Rapids: Eerdmans, 1977), 534-35.

priated related to time of the Church; and the consummated which relates to the second Advent.[47] The following section will explore this threefold eschatological aspect of the antitypical fulfillment using the typological Joseph as a test case. Thus far, this study has investigated the first aspect, the inaugurated eschatology, and it would be beneficial to also explore the appropriated and the consummated eschatological aspects.

Appropriated Eschatology

The second aspect is an ecclesiological fulfillment which is spiritual, universal, and partial. In the same way as each individual or God's people as a whole eventually suffers, it will find its fulfillment collectively and individually among believers. The New Testament states that God will be with His people, as He has promised, for instance in Rom 8:35-39, and He will bless them with the Holy Spirit (Matt 7:11; Luke 11:13; Acts 2:38; Gal 5:22). For Christians, when a person accepts Jesus' offer he or she is adopted into God's royal family (Rom 8:22-25; Eph 1:5). God's people become His witnesses and His tools to bring blessings to the world (Matt 28:18-20; Rev 14:6-12) and their character should reflect that of Joseph and Jesus. Their hardship and suffering, however, will not end until God brings His people home to Heaven (Rev 21:1-5).

Consummated Eschatology

The third aspect will be an apocalyptic, glorious, final, and literal fulfillment. Right before the second coming, Jesus warned there would be a great tribulation (Matt 24:21, 22) and God's people would suffer (Rev 13:11-18). Their loyalty would be tested in a special way, but God would be with His people (Rev 7:3). The suffering would last until the second coming when God puts an end to all evil. In heaven, His people will have an abundance of blessings and they will rule with Him (Rev 20:6). These three aspects, for Christians, bring complete fulfillment to the Joseph oracle and the type of Joseph.

The Threefold Messiah

Each of the three characters—Joseph, Judah, and Levi—was a type of the coming Messiah. In the Jewish tradition, it became an expectation that these would be three unique eschatological messianic figures. In the Chris-

---

[47] For more details, see Davidson's second element in Table 14.

tian tradition, these characters had some similarities, but each individual emphasized a different facet of the Messiah's ministry. Thus, instead of three individuals they were pointing to the same messianic figure, i.e. Jesus Christ.

For Christians, one could argue that the suffering Joseph was a type of the Messiah's first coming. Jesus suffered and died to be the Savior of mankind. Levi, on the other hand, was a type of the coming High Priest. This office foreshadows the role Jesus will play on mankind's behalf in the heavenly temple (Heb 8-10; Rev 1-2). Judah, the Davidic King, points forward to Jesus' everlasting kingdom that will be fully instituted at His second coming. Thus, the Messianic types and their anti-typical fulfillments could be outlined as follows:

1. Messiah ben Joseph—first coming.
2. Messiah ben Levi—High Priest in heaven.
3. Messiah ben Judah—second coming.

Inter-textual Considerations

The inter-textual considerations of the messianic aspects of the Joseph oracle could be a topic for study in itself. However, a few general observations can be made. The concept of the threefold Messiah fits very well with the other messianic passages in the Pentateuch (See for instant Gen 12:1-3; 49:8-12, 22-26; Num 24:15-19; Deut 18:15; 32-33). The first messianic prophecy, recorded in Gen 3:15,[48] is "the 'mother prophecy' that gave birth to all the other promises."[49] This prophecy, as discussed earlier, has the priestly and the suffering elements and it could be argued that the victorious seed of the woman could be pointing to the royal Messiah. The rest of the prophecies in the Pentateuch expand and illuminate the different aspects of this first promise. The Joseph narrative illuminates the suffering element; the

---

[48] This verse has a long messianic tradition both among Jews and conservative Christians (Jacques Doukhan, *On the Way to Emmaus: Five Major Messianic Prophecies Explained* [Clarksville, MD: Lederer Books, 2012], 11-39; Victor P. Hamilton, *The Book of Genesis: Chapters 1-17*, NICOT [Grand Rapids: Eerdmans, 1990], 197-99; and Gordon Wenham, *Genesis 1-15*, WBC 1 [Waco, TX: Word, 1987], 80-81). Already in the third century BCE Jewish rabbis considered it messianic as can be seen in the Septuagint, and in later traditions reflected in Targum Onkelos, Targum Pseudo-Jonathan, Zohar (Zohar, vol. II, folio 120b), and in ancient 'gematria' (Doukhan, *Drinking at the Sources*, 48).

[49] Walter C. Kaiser, Jr, *The Messiah in the Old Testament* (Grand Rapids: Zondervan, 1995), 38.

priesthood and sanctuary service (held and conducted by the tribe of Levi) illuminates the priestly Messiah; and lastly, the kingdom promise given to Judah (Gen 49:8-12) illuminates the royal aspect. Genesis 3:15 is the foundation on which all the other messianic prophecies in the Hebrew Scripture are based, and, for Christians, the New Testament illuminates, even more so, theses aspects of Messiah, by applying them to Christ and His work for humankind. Charles Fritsch writes:

> Joseph is a prophetic type in the truest sense of the word, not because of twenty or thirty dubious resemblances between the life of Joseph and that of Christ, but rather because, in a deeper, spiritual sense, Joseph, by the strength of his faith under testing, by his morally pure character, and by the saving of his people typifies the One who perfectly fulfilled all of these in a life of matchless beauty and perfect obedience that he might obtain for us an eternal redemption.[50]

---

[50] Fritsch, "'God was with Him'," 34.

4. Summary and Conclusion

The poem attributed to Jacob as recorded in Gen 49 reveals what will happen to Jacob's sons in the days to come. This oracle may be divided into twelve oracles, one of which is the oracle given to Joseph. A history of interpretation revealed that the Joseph oracle was considered to be messianic by the rabbis and this passage (among others) was one of the seeds for the Jewish belief in a Messiah ben Joseph. This study also endeavored to provide evidence that Joseph was considered a type of Christ by the Early Church.

The Joseph oracle contains several themes alluding to his life experience and these themes occurred in the following order: being prosperous, suffering, maintaining loyalty because of God's protection, being chosen, blessed, and then receiving elevated social status (princely). An exegesis of the oracle suggests all of these aspects of Joseph's life pointed forward to a future eschatological "Joseph." It also identified the similarities or apparent contradictions between the oracle given to Joseph and the oracle given to Judah. There was sufficient support for there being no contradictions between these two oracles; rather, they foreshadowed different aspects of the coming Messiah. This study endeavored to build upon Richard Davidson's work on defining typology in Scripture and concluded that the Joseph oracle was in fact a typological pointer and that Joseph fits all the characteristics of a type.

If the Joseph oracle can be a typological indicator of Joseph, his life experience could be understood eschatologically. Thus, within a Christian context, it foreshadows the Messiah's agenda at the first coming—he came to suffer and die to be this world's Savior. The Joseph oracle is related to the Judah and Levi oracles in that all refer to different aspects of the Messiah's ministry: Joseph to the first coming, Levi to the Messiah's work as a high priest in heaven, and Judah to the royal Messiah at the second coming. However, within the Jewish context, the Joseph oracle became the seed for the eschatological Messiah ben Joseph—an additional Messianic eschatological figure.

In conclusion, both Jewish and Christian faith communities recognized the typological aspect of the Joseph narrative, however, they interpreted the Messianic aspect differently to fit within their respective religious framework.

APPENDIX 1

**Christological Considerations of Joseph
by the Early Church Fathers**

The early Church Fathers showed great interest in Joseph and viewed him as an example of humility, chastity, and the highest ideal as portrayed in the gospels. They also viewed Joseph as an example of prudent foresight, a prophet, and most importantly, an Old Testament type for Jesus. Following, is a list of references to Joseph found in the literature of the early Church Fathers, which include date, topic, relevant work, and reference to *Patrologia Graeca* (PG) and *Patrologia Latina* (PL).[1]

Joseph as an example of humility

Ambrose of Milan (c. 340-397)	*Ep.* 2.19-22; 37.9-10 (PL 16.884-5; 16.1086)
Augustine (354-430)	*Civ.* 18.4 (PL 41.563)
Gregory the Great (540-604)	*Moral.*, Praef. 6.13 (PL 75. 524B)

Joseph as an example of chastity

Origen (184/5-253/4)	*Cels.* 4.46 (PG 11.1104)
Pseudo-Clement (3rd Century)	*Epistle ad Virgines* 2.8 (PG 1.436)
Zeno of Verona (300-371)	*Tractactus* 1.4 (PL 11.299)
Basil of Caesarea (329/30-379)	*Ep.* 2.3 (PG 32.223C) and 46.4 (PG 32.377A)
Gregory Nazianzus (329-390)	*Orationes Theologicae* 24.13 (PG 35.1184C)
Ambrose of Milan (c. 340-397)	*Exp. Ps. 118* 15.11 (PL 15.1414B)
	Exp. Luc. 3.47 (PL 15.1610B)
	Off. 1.17.66; 2.5.19 (PL 16.43A; 16.108C)
	Exh. Virginit. 13.88 (PL 16.362A)
	Ep. 48.12 (PL 16.1181B)

---

[1] Most of the references from the early Church Fathers in appendix 1 were sourced from Patrick Henry Reardon's article "The Joseph Story: Narrative, Theology, & the Christian Hope," *Touchstone* 9 (1996): 26-30.

Juvencus (330?)	*Genesim* 39 (PL 19.373)
John Chrysostom (c. 349-407)	*Primam ad Thessalonicenses* 4.5 (PG 62.421-2)
	Hom. Gen. 62.4 (PG 54.537-8)
Augustine (354-430)	*Serm.* 318.2; 343.6; 359.3 (PL 38.1439; 39.1509; 39.1592)
Prosper of Aquitaine (c. 390-c.455)	*Carmen de Providentia Divina* 363 (PL 51.625B)
Gregory the Great (540-604)	*Moral.* 6.18.29; 27.10.17; 30.10.38 (PL 75.745C; 76.408B; 76.545-46)

Joseph as an example of prudent foresight

Ambrose of Milan (c. 340-397)	*Off.* 2.16 (PL 16.124-26)
Gregory the Great (540-604)	*Ep.* 35 (PL 77.937C)

Joseph as a Prophet

Origen (184/5-253/4)	*Schol. Matt.* 15.24 (PG 13.1325)
Basil of Caesarea (329/30-379)	*Isaiam, Proem.* 4 (PG 30.125A)
Ambrose of Milan (c. 340-397)	*Jos.* 3.9 (PL 14.676A)
Augustine (354-430)	*Gen. litt.* 12.9.20 (PL 34.461A)
Prosper of Aquitaine (c. 390-c. 455)	*Exp. Ps.* 104 (PL 51.299)
Procopius of Gaza (c. 465-528)	*Isaiam, Proem.* (PG 87.1820)

Joseph as the highest ideal as portrayed in the gospel

Clement of Rome (c. 35-c. 101)	*Prima ad Corinthios* 4 (PG 1.216B)
Cyprian (c. 210-258)	*Pat.* 10 (PL 4.629A)
	Zel. liv. 5 (PL 4.641B-C)
Zeno of Verona (300-371)	Tractactus 1.6 (PL 11.316C)
Cyril of Jerusalem (c. 313-386)	*Catechesis* 8.4 (PG 33.629A)
Ambrose of Milan (c. 340-397)	*Exp. Ps. 118* 11.30 (PL 15.1371-72)
	Off. 1.24.112; 2.11.59; 2.15.7 (PL 16.56D; 16.118B-C; PL 16.112B)

John Chrysostom (c. 349-407)	Secundam ad Thessalonicenses 2.1 (PG 62.471-73)
	Hom. Gen. 63.2 (PG 54.542-43)
Jerome (c. 347-420)	*Comm. Eph.* 3.5 (PL 26.560)

Joseph as a type for Jesus

Eastern Church Fathers

Irenaeus (130-202)	*Iren Fragm.* 17.
Melito of Sardis (2nd Century-180)	*Paschal Homily* 69
Origen (184/5-253/4)	*Hom. Gen.* 15,3; on Gen 45:25-26; 46:4
John Chrysostom (c. 349-407)	*Hom.* 61, on Gen 37 (PG 54.528); *Hom.* 84
Cyril of Alexandria (c. 376-444)	*Genesim* 6.1; 49 (PG 69.285B, 376, 380)
Sophronius of Jerusalem (c. 560-638)	*Triodion* (PG 87.3901C)
Germanus I of Constantinople (c. 634-740)	*Oratio* 1 (PG 98.236-37) and *Oratio* 2 (PG 98.280)

Western Church Fathers

Justin Martyr (c.100-165)	*Dial.* 91.1f (126.1)
Tertullian (c. 155-c. 240)	*Adv. Jud.* 10 (PL 2.626B)
	Marc. 3:18 (PL 2.346)
Hippolytus of Rome (170-235)	*Ben. Is. Jac.* 12; 26
Cyprian (c. 210-258)	*Test.* 1.20 (PL 4.689A)
	Epistula 59, 2
	Pat. 10
	Liber de bono patientiae (PL 4.652-53)
	De Laude Martyrii 29 (PL 4.802B)
Ambrose of Milan (c. 340-397)	*Apol. Dav.* 3.12 (PL 14.856)
	Exp. Ps. 118 16-17; 43 (PL 14.1098-9; 14.1110)
	Jos. 3, 7, 9, 14, 40, 69 (PL 14.673, 675, 676C, 678, 690, 700)
Jerome (347-420)	*Ep. ad Riparium presbyterum*, n.2 (PL 22.908)
Augustine (354-430)	*Epistolarum Classis* 39 (PL 33.919)
	Quaest. Hept. 1:148 (PL 34.588)
	Enarrat. Ps. 80:8 (PL 37.1037); 104:4 (PL 37.1404)
Pseudo-Augustine	*Sermones* 13-16 (PL 39.1765-74) and 93.1 (PL 39.1924)

Gregory the Great (540-604)	*Moral.* 2.36.59 (PL 75.585A)
	Homiliae in Evangelium 2.29.6 (PL 76.1217A)
Bede the Venerable (c. 673-735)	*Gen.* (PL 91.265-66)

Joseph and Jesus started public
ministry at approximately the same age

Origen (184/5-253/4)	*Comm. Ser. Matt.* 78 (PG 13.1727D)

Joseph as a symbol of Jesus' resurrection

Ambrose of Milan (c. 340-397)	*Jos.* 2.7 (PL 14.675)
Rufinus (340/5-410)	*Benedictio Joseph* 2 (PL 21.328).

Kristian S. Heal notes Syriac authors showed significant interest in the Joseph narrative, and viewed Joseph as a type of Christ. His analysis of the Syriac writings and his narrative comparison between Joseph and Jesus, leads Heal to conclude that: "a much broader tradition stands behind this Christological interpretation of the Joseph story."[2] His extensive Table, *Syriac Comparisons of Joseph and Jesus*, provides fifty-seven elements of comparisons based on *Aphrahat* (4th cent. CE), *The Armenian Commentary on Genesis Attributed to Ephrem the Syrian* (306-373 CE), *Sancti patris nostril Ephraem Syri opera omnia, Homilae Mar Narsetis in Joseph* (d. c. 500 CE), and Narsai (d. 503 CE)—to obtain this comprehensive and lengthy list, see Heal, "Joseph as a Type of Christ," 39-45.

---

[2] Kristian S. Heal, "Joseph as a Type of Christ in Syriac Literature," *BYU Studies* 41.1 (2002): 30.

APPENDIX 2

Kingdom Prophecies and Eschatology

Many of the prophecies from the classical prophets concerning the Messianic Kingdom are couched within the framework of the covenant relationship. Israel's response to the covenant would determine the outcome of the prophecy. If they stayed loyal to the covenant, blessings were poured upon them, but unfaithfulness reaped the curses (Deut 4 and 27-28 give some examples of the promised curses and blessings).

From this, one could conclude that prophecies have two different outcomes. The first, the covenant blessings were God's original plan for Israel and fulfilled the prophecy in its literal form. The second, the covenant curses would bring judgment and possible rejection upon Israel. In this way, the prophecies are conditional in nature. But it is important to note that the messianic prophecies are in themselves unconditional. The Messiah will come regardless of the spiritual state of His people.

All the Old Testament prophecies and types were intended to be fulfilled in history as this was God's original plan for national and ethnic Israel—God's chosen people. God's intention was that the prophecies should have been literally fulfilled. The New Testament and the Christian Church claims Israel, and by extension Judaism, did not stay faithful and the religious leaders rejected God as their king (Matt 23:38).[1]

---

[1] This view became the foundation for Christian replacement theology—that the Christians replaced the Jewish people as God's chosen people. Following this theology, it would be the Christian believers who would inherit all the biblical promises of the Old Testament, while the curses are often still viewed as applicable to the Jewish faith community. Additionally, the essence of Old Testament prophecies would also be applied to Christian believers as they consider themselves the New Spiritual people.

The reader should keep in mind, however, that this view was not originally anti-Semitic as the first Christians were all Jews. This changed when the Christian movement became largely a Gentile church and they no longer considered themselves a part of the Jewish people. There were many Jewish sects during Second Temple period Judaism, and the early Christian sect's self-understanding had a lot in

Matthew portrays Christ as the new Israel by paralleling Matthew 1-4 with the Exodus narrative of the Pentateuch. Christ came out from Egypt, was baptized, and finally was in the wilderness for 40 days—this parallel the experience of the people of Israel who were brought out Egypt, went through the Red Sea, and wondered through the wilderness for 40 years. It is also interesting to note the parallel between the Sermon of the Mount (Matt 5-7), and the giving of the Torah.

According to the Christian narrative, at the crucifixion, everyone except Jesus turned against God. He was the only faithful Israelite, the true remnant. Therefore, God made Him the cornerstone on which the spiritual Israel would be built. Through Christ, the new Israel, all the prophecies would be fulfilled. By accepting Christ as Savior, a believing individual would become a part of Him, a part of the spiritual Israel (Eph 2:14-18; 5:30). God's Church represents the spiritual Israel, since it is a congregation of believers, and would receive the fulfillment of all kingdom prophecies (Gal 3:29; 6:16). In the aspect dealing with spiritual Israel, the prophecies would be partially fulfilled in a spiritual and universal sense. There would also be a third aspect of fulfillment at the end of history, at Christ's second coming. This would be a glorious, universal, literal, and final fulfillment.

From this, it can be concluded that the Old Testament kingdom prophecies of classical prophets have one eschatological (last day) fulfillment with three aspects. The first aspect is inaugurated eschatology which has its climax in Christ's life and work at the first advent. The second aspect is appropriated eschatology which is partly fulfilled in the Church between the first and the second advents. The last aspect is consummated eschatology which will take place at the second advent and onwards in a literal and universal sense. These aspects of fulfillment are differentiated according to the physical or spiritual presence of Christ. The Christian perspective and principles outlined above are at the foundation of Davidson's interpretation of bib-

---

common with that of the Qumran community. Like the Qumran community, the followers of Jesus Christ considered themselves the true covenant people, a true remnant people who believed they were the last generation. Both communities utilized a *pesher* reading of ancient prophecies and believed the TaNakh carried a message specifically for their community. Both communities believed only their members would be saved. Jeremiah's new covenant oracle (Jer 31:30-34) was central for both communities, however, the most unique aspect of Christianity, setting it apart from other Second Temple period sects, was their claim of possessing a completely new and different covenant which replaced the one given to Israel by God at Mt. Sinai.

lical types. Charts 1-3 provides a visual illustration of Davidson's typological approach.

Chart 1, "The eschatological substructure of biblical typology," shows the eschatological substructure of the New Testament based on the three distinct fulfillment phases of Old Testament prophecies and types: inaugurated/Christological, appropriated/ecclesiological, and consummated/apocalyptic fulfillment. It also provides four type-antitype examples: Adam (person), Noahic Flood and Exodus (events), and Sanctuary/Temple (institution).

Chart 2, "Typological interpretation of the Old Testament: Prophetic indicators identifying the Old Testament types," provides eight examples of Old Testament types (person [x5]—Adam, Moses, Joshua, David, and Jonah; event [x2]—Flood and Exodus; institution [x1]—Earthly Sanctuary) which are identified as typological not only within the immediate context (a typological indicator or control) but also indicators in later Old Testament texts. This chart also provides the New Testament announcement of antitype for each of these eight Old Testament types examples.

Chart 3, "The four-fold substructure of biblical typology: Examples from Israel typology," focuses on Old Testament types related to the institutions (Temple), offices (priesthood, kings, prophets), and historical events related to the nation of Israel and the four-fold substructure of biblical typology (historical, Christological, ecclesiological, and apocalyptic).

Chart 1. The eschatological substructure of biblical typology

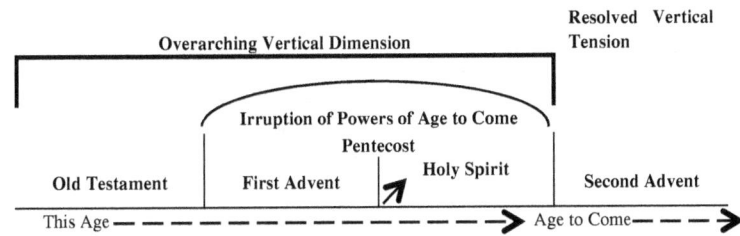

	CLASSICAL PROPHECY			
In Kingdom Language	OT Kingdom Prophecies	Christ's First Advent*	Time of Christian Church	Christ's Second Advent**
	Theocratic Kingdom (Direct Rule by God or His Earthly Vicegerent	Kingdom of Grace (Matt 12:28; Heb 4:16)	Tension Between "Already" and "Not Yet" (Matt 16:19)	Kingdom of Glory (Matt 25:31)
In Eschatological Language	Verbal Predictions of End Time	Inaugurated Eschatology	Appropriated Eschatology	Consummated Eschatology
Fulfillment Mode	National, Ethnic	Literal, Local Fulfillment	Spiritual, Universal, Partial Fulfillment	Glorious, Final Literal Fulfillment
	TYPOLOGY			
Typological Fulfillment Aspects	Old Testament Types	New Testament Antitypes		
	Person, Events, Institutions	Christ (Christological)	Church (Ecclesiological)	Final Climax (Apocalyptic)
Fulfillment Mode	National, Ethnic	Literal, Local Fulfillment	Spiritual, Universal, Partial Fulfillment	Glorious, Final Literal Fulfillment
Example (1)	Adam	Christ the Second Adam (Mark 1:13; Rom 5:12-21)	Christians – New Humanity (Eph 4:24)	Christ as Last Adam (1 Cor 15:42-49; Heb 2:6-9)

Chart 1 – *Continued*

Aspects	Old Testament Types	New Testament Antitypes		
Example (2)	Noahic Flood	Christ's Flood Experience – Death and Resurrection (1 Pet 3:18-21; Mark 10:38-39)	Believer's Flood Experience – Sacrament of Baptism (1 Pet 3:18-21)	Apocalyptic Flood – Global Destruction of the World (Matt 24:37-39; Luke 17:26-27; 2 Pet 2:5-9; 3:5-7)
(3)	Exodus	Christ's Exodus (Matt 1-5; Luke 9:31)	Spiritual Exodus (Heb 4; 2 Cor 6:17)	Apocalyptic Exodus (Rev 15:1-3)
(4)	Sanctuary/Temple	Christ as Temple (John 1:14; 2:21; Matt 12:6)	Church as Temple (1 Cor 3:16, 17; 2 Cor 6:16)	Heavenly Temple/Ultimate Temple (Rev 3:12; 7:15; 11:19; 21:3, 22)

*See 1 Cor 10:11 "end of ages"; Heb 1:2 "these last days"; 1 Pet 1:20 "end of times."
**See 1 Cor 15:24 "end"; Heb 9:28 "second time"' 1 Pet 1:5 "last time."

Source: Davidson, "Eschatological Hermeneutic of Biblical Typology," 37-38.

Chart 2. Typological interpretation of the Old Testament: Prophetic indicators identifying the Old Testament types.

OT Type (Person/Event/Institution)	OT Verbal Indicator of Typology	NT Announcement of Antitype
1. Adam Genesis 1–5	**New Adam** Immediate context: Gen 1:26–27; 2:5–7, 18–23; 3:15, 17; 5:1–2 (corporate solidarity of Adam with "humanity" and with the Messianic seed) Later OT indicators: Ps 8:4–8; Dan 7:13–14	**Antitypical Adam** Rom 5:12–21; 1 Cor15:21–22, 45–49; Heb 2:6–8; cf. Matt 24:30; 26:64; etc.
2. Flood Genesis 6–9	**New Cosmic Judgment/Salvation** Immediate Context: Gen 6:13; 7:23; 8:1 (See Warren Gage, *The Gospel in Genesis* [Winona Lake: Carpenter, 1984], 7–16.) Later OT indicators: Isa 24:18; 28:2; 43:2; 54:8–9; Nah 1:8; Dan 9:26	**Antitype of the Flood** 1 Pet 3:18–21; cf. Matt 24:37–39; Luk e 17:26–27; 2 Pet 2:5, 9; 3:5–7
3. Exodus Exodus – Numbers	**New Exodus** Immediate Context: Exod15:14–17; Numbers 23–24 (esp. 23:22; 24:8, 14–17; See Sailhamer, *The Pentateuch as Narrative*, 408.). Later OT indicators: Hos 2:14–15; 12:9, 13; 13:4–5; Jer 23:4–8; 16:14–15; 31:32; Isa 11:15–16; 35; 40:3–5; 41:17–20; 42:14–16; 43:1–3, 14–21; 48:20–21; 49:8–12; 51:9–11; 52:3–6, 11–12; 55:12–13 (See C. H. Dodd, According to the Scriptures [London: Nisbet, 1952], 75–133; Friedbert Ninow, Indicators of Typology within the Old Testament: the Exodus Motif [Frankfort am Main, New York: P. Lang, 2001], passim.)	**Antitypical Exodus** 1 Cor 10: 1–13; cf. Matt 1–5; Luke 9:31; etc. (See Richard M. Davidson, *Typology in Scripture: A Study of Hermeneutical τύπος Structures* [AUSDDS 2; Berrien Springs, MI: Andrews University Press, 1981],193–297; George Balentine, "The Concept of the New Exodus in the Gospels" [Th.D. diss., Southern Baptist Theological Seminary, 1961].)

Chart 2 - Continued

OT Type (Person/Event/Institution)	OT Verbal Indicator of Typology	NT Announcement of Antitype
4. Earthly Sanctuary Exodus 25–40	**Earthly a Copy of the Heavenly Sanctuary** Immediate context: Exod 25:9,40; Later OT indicators: Pss 11:4; 18:6; 60:8; 63:2; 68:35; 96:6; 102:19; 150:1; Isa 6; Jonah 2:7; Mic 1:2; Hab 2:20; etc. (See Davidson, *Typology in Scripture*, 367–388; Elias Brasil de Souza, *The Heavenly Sanctuary/Temple Motif in the Hebrew Bible: Function and Relationship to the Earthly Counter Parts* [ATSDS 7; Berrien Springs, MI: ATS Publications, 2006], passim.)	**Antitypical Heavenly Sanctuary** Heb 8:5; 9:24; cf. Rev 8:1–5; 11:19; 16:1; etc.
5. Moses Pentateuch	**New Moses** Immediate context: Deut 18:15–19 Later OT indicator: Deut 34:10 (Added probably by Ezra; see Sailhamer, *The Pentateuch as Narrative*, 456, 478–479).	**Antitypical Moses** John 1:21; 6:14; 8:40; etc.
6. Joshua The Book of Joshua	**New Joshua** Immediate context: Exod 23:23; Num 13:8, 16; 27:17, 21; Deut 3:28; 18:15–17; 31:3, 23; 34:10–12; Josh 1:2–5; 3:7; 4:14 (Joshua does the same work as the Angel of the Lord, and of Moses, but is clearly not the New Moses) Later OT indicator: Isa 49:8 (the Messiah does the same work as Joshua in Deut 31:7; Josh 1:6) (See Richard M. Davidson, *In the Footsteps of Joshua* [Hagerstown, Md.: Review and Herald, 1995], 24–35.)	**Antitypical Joshua** Hebrews 4; cf. Matt 11:28; Eph 1:11, 14, 18; Col 2:15; 3:24; Heb 1:4; 9:15; 12:22–24

Chart 2 – Continued

OT Type (Person/Event/Institution)	OT Verbal Indicator of Typology	NT Announcement of Antitype
7. David The Psalms	**New David** Immediate Context: Ps 2 (esp. v. 12); 16:8–11; 22; 40:6–8; etc. (language goes beyond historical David) Later OT indicators: Jer 23:5; Ezek 34:23; 37:24; Dan 9:26 (echoing Ps 22:11); Isa 9:5, 6; 11:1–5; Hos 3:5; Amos 9:11; Zech 8:3; etc. (See Richard M. Davidson, "New Testament Use of the Old Testament," JATS 5 [1994]: 23–28.)	**Antitypical David** Matt 1:1–18 (14 is the gematria number of David); John 19:24; Acts 2:29–33; 13:31–37; Heb 1:5; 5:5; 10:5–9; etc.
8. Jonah The Book of Jonah	**New Jonah** Immediate context: Jonah 1:17; 2:2, 6 (death-resurrection language, 3 days/nights; description goes beyond historical Jonah) Later OT indicators: Hos 6:1–3 (= Israel's death-resurrection experience, third day); Hos 7:11 (Israel is like silly "Jonah" [dove]); Isa 41–53 (Messiah represents and recapitulates experience of Israel, especially in death-resurrection) Isa 41:8; 42:1; 44:1; 49:3–6; 52:13–53:11; etc.) (See Davidson, "NT Use of OT," 29–30.)	**Antitypical Jonah** Matt 12:39–41; 16:4; Luke 11:29–32;

Source: Davidson, "Eschatological Hermeneutic of Biblical Typology," 19-23.

Chart 3. The four-fold substructure of biblical typology: Examples from Israel typology

Historical	Christological	Ecclesiological	Apocalyptic
Institutions and Office			
Temple	Antitypical temple (John 1:14; 2:21; Matt 12:6)	Spiritual temple (1 Cor 3:16, 17; 2 Cor 6:16)	Apocalyptic temple (Rev 3:12; 11:19)
Priesthood	Antitypical (high) Priest (Heb 3:1; 6:20; 8:1)	Priesthood of believers (1 Pet 2:9; Rev 1:5)	Priests of God (Rev 20:6)
Kings	Antitypical King (Matt 12:42; 21:5)	Royal nation (1 Pet 2:9)	Saints reign forever (Rev 22:5)
Prophets	Antitypical Prophet (Matt 12:41; 13:12-15)	Prophesying Church (Acts 2:17; Eph 4:11)	Prophesying remnant (Rev 12:17; 19:10)
Historical Events			
Exodus	Christ's Exodus (Matt 2:15; Luke 9:31)	Spiritual Exodus of Church (Heb 4; Isa 52:4, 11; 2 Cor 6:17)	Final Exodus to heaven (Rev 15:1-3)
Baptism in Red Sea (1 Cor 10:1-2)	Christ's baptism (Matt 3)	Spiritual Israel's baptism (Rom 6:4; Col 2:12)	[Apocalyptic baptism] (Rev 15:3; Mark 10:38)
Covenant at Sinai	New Covenant (Mark 14:24)	Continues in Church (Heb 8:6-13; 10:4-18; 12:24)	Ark of testament open (Rev 11:19)
Temptation in Wilderness	Christ's temptations (Matt 4; Luke 4)	"Wilderness temptations" (1 Cor 10:5-14)	Great Tribulation (Rev 7:14) Hour of temptation (Rev 3:10)
Gathered to Jerusalem (for feasts; after Exile; after Exodus)	Christ's gathering of disciples (John 10:14-16; 11:52; Matt 12:30)	Gathered to heavenly Jerusalem (Heb 12:22)	Gathered to New Jerusalem (Rev 21-22; Matt 24:31; 2 Thess 2:1; Luke 13:28-29)
Enemies gathered against Israel	Enemies gathered against Christ (John 13:18; 15:25; Acts 1:20)	Spiritual Enemies against the Church (Rev 14:20; 16:14-16)	Literal gathering of enemies against New Jerusalem (Rev 20:8, 9)

Source: Richard M. Davidson,"The Nature of Biblical Typology—Crucial Issues," paper presented at the 48th Annual Meeting of the Midwest Regional Evangelical Theological Society, St. Paul, Minnesota, 14 March 2003.

BIBLIOGRAPHY

Aberbach, Moses. "Joseph: In the Aggadah." *EncJud* 11:410-11.

_____, and Bernard Grossfeld. *Targum Onkelos To Genesis*. Based on A. Sperber's edition. Denver: Ktav, 1982.

Albright, William F. "From the Patriarchs to Moses." *BA* 36.1 (February 1973): 5-33.

Alexander, P. "3 (Hebrew Apocalypse of) Enoch: A New Translation and Introduction." Pages 223-302 in vol. 1 of *The Old Testament Pseudepigrapha*. Edited by James H. Charlesworth. New York: Doubleday, 1983.

Alexander, T. Desmond. "Messianic Ideology in the Book of Genesis." Pages 19-39 in *The Lord's Anointed: Interpretation of Old Testament Messianic Texts*. Edited by Philip E. Satterthwaite, Richard S. Hess, and Gordon J. Wenham. Grand Rapids: Baker, 1995.

Alexander, T. D. "From Adam to Judah: The Significance of the Family Tree in Genesis." *EvQ* 61.1 (January 1989): 5-19.

Aling, Charles. "Some Remarks on the Historicity of the Joseph Story." *NEASB* 39-40 (1995): 31-39.

Allegro, J.M. "A Possible Mesopotamian Background to the Joseph Blessing of Gen.xlix." *ZAW* 64 (1952): 249-51.

Alter, Robert. *Genesis: Translation and Commentary*. New York: Norton, 1996.

_____. *The Art of Biblical Narrative*. New York: Basic Books, 1981.

Aptowitzer, V. "Asenath, the Wife of Joseph: A Haggadic Literary-Historical Study." *HUCA* 1 (1924): 239-306.

Archer, Gleason L, Jr. *A Survey of Old Testament Introduction*. Chicago: Moody, 1994.

Armerding, Carl. "The Last Words of Jacob: Genesis 49." *BSac* 112 (1955): 320-9.

Baron, David. *The Visions and Prophecies of Zechariah: The Prophet of Hope and of Glory*. London: Morgan & Scott, 1919.

Battenfield, James R. "Hebrew Stylistic Development in Archaic Poetry: A Textual-Critical and Exegetical Study of the Blessing of Jacob, Genesis 49:1-27." PhD diss., Grace College, 1976.

Bellett, J.C. *God's Witness in Prophecy and History: Bible Studies on the Historical Fulfillment of Jacob's Prophetic Blessings on the Twelve Tribes Contained in Gen. XLIX.* London: J. Master, 1884.

Bennetch, John H. "The Prophecy of Jacob." *BSac* 95 (1938): 417-35.

Blenkinsopp, J. "The Oracle of Judah and the Messianic Entry." *JBL* 80 (1961): 55-64.

Blidstein, Gerald J. "Messiah in Rabbinic Thought." *EncJud* 14:112-3.

Braude, William G., ed. *Pesikta Rabbati: Discourses for Feasts, Fasts, and Special Sabbaths.* 2 vols. Translated by William G. Braude. YJS 18. New Haven: Yale University Press, 1968.

Brenton, Lancelot C.L. *The Septuagint with Apocrypha: Greek and English.* Peabody, MA: Hendrickson, 1995.

Brown, Francis, with S.R. Driver and Charles A. Briggs. *A Hebrew and English Lexicon of the Old Testament with an Appendix Containing the Biblical Aramaic.* Based on the lexicon of William Gesenius. Oxford: Clarendon, 1952.

Buchanan, George Wesley. "Eschatology and the 'End of Days.'" *JNES* 20 (1961): 188-93.

Burchard, Christoph. "Das Lamm in der Waagschale: Herkunft und Hintergrund eines haggadischen Midraschs zu Ex 1:15-22." *ZNW* 57 (1966): 219-28.

———. "Joseph and Aseneth: A New Translation and Introduction." Pages 177-247 in vol. 2 of *The Old Testament Pseudepigrapha.* Edited by James H. Charlesworth. New York: Doubleday, 1985.

Candlish, Robert S. *Commentary on Genesis.* CCL 2. Grand Rapids: Zondervan, 1955.

Candlish, Robert S. *Studies in Genesis.* Grand Rapids: Kregel, 1979.

Casselli, Stephen J. "Jesus as Eschatological Torah." *TJ* 18.1 (1997): 15-41.

Charlesworth, James H. "In the Crucible: The Pseudepigrapha as Biblical Interpretation." Pages 20-43 in vol. 14 of *The Pseudepigrapha and Early Biblical Interpretation.* Edited by James H. Charlesworth and Craig A. Evans. Sheffield: JSOT Press, 1993.

———. *The Old Testament Pseudepigrapha and the New Testament: Prolegomena for the Study of Christian Origins.* SNTSMS 54. New York: Cambridge University Press, 1985.

_____, ed. *The Messiah: Developments in Earliest Judaism and Christianity*. Minneapolis: Fortress, 1992.

_____, ed. *The Old Testament Pseudepigrapha*. 2 vols. New York: Doubleday, 1983-1985.

Charlesworth, James H., and P. Dykers. *Pseudepigrapha and Modern Research*. SCS 7. Missoula, MT: Scholars Press for the Society of Biblical Literature, 1976.

Charlesworth, James H., and Craig A. Evans, eds. *The Pseudepigrapha and Early Biblical Interpretation*. JSPSup 14. Sheffield: JSOT Press, 1993.

Chesnutt, Randall D. "The Social Setting and Purpose of Joseph and Aseneth." *JSP* 2 (1988): 21-48.

Coats, George W. "The Joseph Story and Ancient Wisdom: A Reappraisal." *CBQ* 35 (1973): 285-97.

Cohen, A., ed. *Sotah*. London: Soncino Press, 1936.

Cohen, Norman J. *Self, Struggle and Change: Family Conflict Stories in Genesis and Their Healing Insights for Our Lives*. Woodstock, VT: Jewish Lights Publishing, 1995.

Coleman, Gillis Byrns. "The Phenomenon of Christian Interpolations into Jewish Apocalyptic Texts: A Bibliographical Survey and Methodological Analysis." PhD diss., Vanderbilt University, 1976.

Craigie, Peter C. *The Book of Deuteronomy*. NICOT. Grand Rapids: Eerdmans, 1976.

Cross, Frank M., Jr., and David Noel Freedman. "The Blessing of Moses." *JBL* 67 (1948): 191-210.

_____. *Studies in Ancient Yahwistic Poetry*. 2nd ed. Biblical Resource Series. Grand Rapids: Eerdmans, 1975.

Culbertson, Philip. "Blessing Jacob's Sons, Inheriting Family Myths." *STRev* 37 (1993): 52-76.

Dahood, M. "Is 'Eben Yisra'el a Divine Title? (Gen 49, 24)." *Bib* 40 (1959): 1002-7.

Davidson, Richard M. "Corporative Solidarity in the Old Testament." TMs, Andrews University, 1997.

_____. "Interpreting Scripture: An Hermeneutical 'Decalogue.'" *JATS* 4.2 (1993): 95-114.

_____. *Principles of Biblical Interpretation*. TMs, Andrews University, 1995.

_____. "The Authority of Scripture: A Personal Pilgrimage." *JATS* 1.1 (1990): 39-56.

_____. "The Eschatological Hermeneutic of Biblical Typology." *TheoRhēma* 6.2 (2011): 5-48.

_____. "The Eschatological Literary Structure of the Old Testament." Pages 349-66 in *Creation, Life, Hope: Essays in Honor of Jacques B. Doukhan*. Edited by Jiří Moskala. Berrien Springs, MI: Old Testament Department, Seventh-day Adventist Theological Seminary, Andrews University, 2000.

_____. "The Nature of Biblical Typology—Crucial Issues." Paper presented at the 48th Annual Meeting of the Midwest Regional Evangelical Theological Society, St. Paul, Minnesota, 14 March 2003.

_____. *Typology in Scripture: A Study of Hermeneutical τύπος Structures*. Andrews University Seminary Doctoral Dissertation Series. Berrien Springs, MI: Andrews University Press, 1981.

Davidson, Robert. *Genesis 12-50*. The Cambridge Bible Commentary. New York: Cambridge University Press, 1979.

Davis, John J. *Paradise to Prison: Studies in Genesis*. Grand Rapids: Baker, 1989.

De Jonge, Marinus. "Christian Influence in the Testaments of the Twelve Patriarchs." *NovT* 4.3 (July 1960): 182-235.

_____. "Messiah." *ABD* 4:777-88.

_____. "Once More: Christian Influence in the Testaments of the Twelve Patriarchs." *NovT* 5.4 (Nov 1962): 311-9.

_____, ed. *Studies on the Testaments of the Twelve Patriarchs: Text and Interpretation*. SVTP 3. Leiden: Brill, 1975.

_____. *The Testament of the Twelve Patriarchs: A Study of Their Text, Composition and Origin*. Assen: Van Gorcum, 1953.

Deane, William J. *Pseudepigrapha: An Account of Certain Apocryphal Sacred Writings of the Jews and Early Christians*. Edinburgh: T&T Clark, 1891.

Dix, G.H. "Notes and Studies: The Messiah Ben Joseph." *JTS* 28 (1925-26): 130-43.

Donaldson, Mara E. "Kinship Theory in the Patriarchal Narratives: The Case of the Barren Wife." *JAAR* 49.1 (March 1981): 77-87.

Douglas, Rees Conrad. "Liminality and Conversion in Joseph and Aseneth." *JSP* 3 (1988): 31-42.

Doukhan, Jacques B. *Drinking at the Sources: An Appeal to the Jew and the Christian to Note Their Common Beginnings*. Translated by Walter R. Beach and Robert M. Johnston. Mountain View, CA: Pacific Press, 1981.

_____. *One the Way to Emmaus: Five Major Messianic Prophecies Explained*. Clarksville, MD: Lederer Books, 2012.

Driver, S R. *The Book of Genesis: With Introduction and Notes by S. R. Driver*. 15th ed. WC. London: Methuen, 1954.

Easterly, Ellis. "A Case of Mistaken Identity: The Judges in Judges Don't Judge." *BRev* 13.2 (April 1997): 41-43, 47.

Elgvin, Torleif. "4Q474 — A Joseph Apocryphon?" *RevQ* 18 (1997): 97-107.

Emerton, J. A. "Some Difficult Words in Genesis 49." Pages 81-93 in *Words and Meanings*. Edited by Peter R. Ackroyd and Barnabas Lindars. Cambridge: Cambridge University Press, 1968.

Epstein, I., ed. *Sukkah*. The Babylonian Talmud. London: Soncino Press, 1938.

Etheridge, John W. *The Targums of Onkelos and Jonathan Ben Uzziel on the Pentateuch: Genesis and Exodus*. London: Longman, Green, Longman, and Roberts, 1862.

Evans, Craig A. "Messiah." *EDSS* 1:537-42.

_____, and Peter W. Flint, eds. *Eschatology, Messianism, and the Dead Sea Scrolls*. Grand Rapids: Eerdmans, 1997.

Ezra, Ibn. *Ibn Ezra's Commentary on the Pentateuch: Genesis (Bereshit)*. Translated by H. Norman Strickman and Arthur M. Silver. New York: Menorah Publishing Company, 1988.

_____. *Rabbi Abraham Ibn Ezra's Commentary on Books 3-5 of Psalms: Chapters 73-150*. Translated and Annotated by H. Norman Strickman. New York: Touro College Press; Brighton, MA: Academic Studies Press, 2016.

Fairbairn, Patrick. *Typology of Scripture*. 2 vols. Grand Rapids: Kregel, 1989.

Fishbane, Michael. *Biblical Interpretation in Ancient Israel*. New York: Clarendon Press - Oxford, 1985.

Flusser, David. "Messianism: Second Temple Period." *EncJud* 14:111-12.

Freedman, H., and Maurice Simon, eds. *Midrash Rabbah*. 10 vols. London: Soncino Press, 1983.

Fripp, Edgar Innes. "Note on Gen. XLIX, 24b-26." *ZAW* 11 (1891): 262-66.

Fritsch, Charles T. "'God Was with Him': A Theological Study of the Joseph Narrative." *Int* 9 (1955): 21-34.

———. "Pseudepigrapha." *IDB* 3:960-64.

Furman, Nelly. "His Story Versus Her Story: Male Genealogy and Female Strategy in the Jacob Cycle." *Semeia* 46 (1989): 141-49.

Gevirtz, Stanley. "The Life Spans of Joseph and Enoch and the Parallelism." *JBL* 96 (1977): 570-71.

———. "Of Patriarchs and Puns: Joseph at the Fountain, Jacob at the Ford." *HUCA* 46 (1975): 33-54.

Glenny, W. Edward. "Typology: A Summary of the Present Evangelical Discussion." *JETS* 40 (1997): 627-38.

Goldin, Judah. "The Youngest Son or Where Does Genesis 38 Belong." *JBL* 96 (1977): 27-44.

Green, W. Henry. "The Pentateuchal Question. III. Gen. 37:2-Ex. 12:51." *Hebraica* 7.1 (1890): 1-38.

Greenstone, Julius H. *The Messiah Idea in Jewish History*. Philadelphia: Jewish Publication Society of America, 1906.

Gugliotto, Lee J. *Handbook for Bible Study: A Guide to Understand, Teaching, and Preaching the Word of God*. Hagerstown, MD: Review & Herald, 1995.

Gunkel, Hermann. *Genesis*. Translated by Mark E. Biddle. Macon, GA: Mercer University Press, 1997.

Guyot, Gilmore H. "Messianism in the Book of Genesis." *CBQ* 13 (1951): 415-21.

Hale, John G. "Exegesis of Genesis XLIX, 22-26." *The Congregational Quarterly* 17 (1875): 506-14.

Hamilton, James M. Jr. "Was Joseph a Type of the Messiah? Tracing the Typological Identification Between Joseph, David, and Jesus." *SBJT* 12.4 (2008): 52-77.

Hamilton, Victor P. *The Book of Genesis: Chapters 1-17*. NICOT. Grand Rapids: Eerdmans, 1990.

———. *The Book of Genesis: Chapters 18-50*. NICOT. Grand Rapids: Eerdmans, 1995.

Hasel, Gerhard F. *Biblical Interpretation Today*. Silver Spring, MD: Biblical Research Institute, 1985.

Hayes, John H., and J. Maxwell Miller, eds. *Israelite and Judaean History*. OTL. Philadelphia: Westminster, 1977.

Kristian S. Heal, "Joseph as a Type of Christ in Syriac Literature," *BYU Studies* 41.1 (2002): 29-49.

Heard, W.J., and C.A. Evans. "Revolutionary Movements, Jewish." Pages 936-947 in *Dictionary of New Testament Background*. Edited by Craig A. Evans and Stanley E. Porter. Downers Grove, IL: InterVarsity Press, 2000.

Heaton, E.W. "The Joseph Saga." *ExpTim* 59 (1947): 134-36.

Heck, Joel D. "A History of Interpretation of Genesis 49 and Deuteronomy 33." *BSac* 147 (1990): 16-31.

Heineman, Joseph. "The Messiah of Ephraim and the Premature Exodus of the Tribe of Ephraim." Pages 339-53 in *Messianism in the Talmudic Era*. Edited by Leo Landman. New York: Ktav, 1979.

Hengstenberg, Ernst W. *Christology of the Old Testament, and a Commentary on the Messianic Predictions*. Grand Rapids: Kregel Publications, 1970.

Herr, Moshe David. "Midrash." *EncJud* 14:182-185.

Hertz, J.H., ed. *The Pentateuch and Haftorahs: Hebrew Text, English Translation and Commentary*. London: Soncino Press, 1969.

Hilgert, Earle. "The Dual Image of Joseph in Hebrew and Early Jewish Literature." *PCSBR* 30 (1985): 5-21.

Himmelfarb, Martha. *Jewish Messiahs in the Christian Empire: A History of the Book of Zerubbabel*. Cambridge: Harvard University Press, 2017.

―――――. "The Messiah Son of Joseph in Ancient Judaism." Pages 771-90 in vol. 2 of *Envisioning Judaism: Studies in Honor of Peter Schäfer on the Occasion of his Seventieth Birthday*. Edited By Raʿanan S. Boustan, Klaus Herrmann, Reimund Leicht, Annette Yoshiko Reed, and Giuseppe Veltri with the collaboration of Alex Ramos. Tübingen: Mohr Siebeck, 2013.

Hollander, Harm W. *Joseph as an Ethical Model in the Testaments of the Twelve Patriarchs*. SVTP 6. Leiden: Brill, 1981.

―――――, and Marinus de Jonge. *The Testaments of the Twelve Patriarchs: A Commentary*. SVTP 8. Leiden: Brill, 1985.

Holtz, Barry. "Midrash." Pages 177-212 in *Back to the Sources: Reading the Classic Jewish Texts*. Edited by Barry W. Holtz. New York: Simon & Schuster, 1984.

Holtz, Traugott. "Christliche Interpolation in Joseph und Aseneth." *NTS* 14 (1968): 482-97.

Horbury, W. "The Messianic Associations of 'The Son of Man.'" *JTS* 36.1 (April 1985): 34-55.
Horsley, Richard A. "Messianic Movements in Judaism." *ABD* 4:791-97.
Isaac, E. "The Ethiopic History of Joseph: Translation with Introduction and Notes." *JSP* 6 (1990): 3-125.
Isaacson, Irvin. "The Other Messiah: The Story of the Messiah ben Joseph." PhD diss., Jewish Teachers Seminary and People's University, 1981.
Jones, Alfred. *Jones' Dictionary of Old Testament Proper Names*. Grand Rapids: Kregel, 1997.
Judaeus, Philo. *The Works of Philo: Complete and Unabridged*. Translated by C. D. Yonge. Peabody, MA: Hendrickson, 1993.
Jukes, Andrew. *Types in Genesis*. Grand Rapids: Kregel, 1976.
Kaiser, Walter C., Jr. *The Messiah in the Old Testament*. Grand Rapids: Zondervan, 1995.
_____. *Toward an Old Testament Theology*. Grand Rapids: Zondervan, 1978.
_____. *Toward an Exegetical Theology*. Grand Rapids: Baker, 1981.
_____. *Toward Rediscovering the Old Testament*. Grand Rapids: Zondervan, 1987.
Kee, H. C. "Testament of the Twelve Patriarchs: A New Translation and Introduction." Pages 775-828 in vol. 1 of *Old Testament Pseudepigrapha*. Edited by James Charlesworth. New York: Doubleday, 1983.
Keil, C.F., and F. Delitzsch. *The Pentateuch*. Translated by James Martin. COT 1. Edinburgh: T&T Clark, 1872.
Kidner, Derek. *Genesis: An Introduction and Commentary*. TOTC 1. Chicago: InterVarsity Press, 1967.
Kimchi, David. *Rabbi David Kimchi's Commentary upon the Prophecies of Zechariah*. Translated by A. M'Caul. London: James Duncan, 1837.
King, J. Robin. "The Joseph Story and Divine Politics: A Comparative Study of a Biographic Formula from the Ancient Near East." *JBL* 106 (1987): 577-94.
Klausner, Joseph. *The Messianic Idea in Israel: From Its Beginning to the Completion of the Mishnah*. Translated by W.F. Stinespring. New York: Macmillan, 1955.
Klein, William W., Craig L. Blomberg, and Robert L. Hubbard, Jr. *Introduction to Biblical Interpretation*. Dallas, TX: Word, 1993.
Knohl, Israel. *The Messiah before Jesus: The Suffering Servant of the Dead Sea Scrolls*. Berkeley: University of California Press, 2000.

Koch, Klaus. "Das Lamm, das Ägypten vernichtet: Ein Fragment aus Jannes und Jambres und sein geschichtlicher Hintergrund." *ZNW* 57 (1966): 79-93.

Kosmala, Hans. "At the End of the Days." Pages 302-312 in *Messianism in the Talmudic Era*. Edited by Leo Landman. New York: Ktav, 1979.

Kugel, James L. *In Potiphar's House: The Interpretive Life of Biblical Texts*. San Francisco: HarperCollins, 1990.

Ladd, George Eldon. "Apocalyptic Literature." *IDB* 1:151-61.

Landman, Leo, ed. *Messianism in the Talmudic Era*. New York: Ktav, 1979.

Layton, Scott C. "The Steward in Ancient Israel: A Study of Hebrew (ÁSER)'AL-Habbayit in Its Near Eastern Setting." *JBL* 109 (1990): 633-49.

Liver, J. "The Doctrine of the Two Messiahs in Sectarian Literature in the Time of the Second Commonwealth." *HTR* 52 (1959): 149-85.

Lockshine, Martin I. *Rabbi Samuel Ben Meir's Commentary on Genesis: An Annotated Translation*. Jewish Studies 5. Lewiston, NY: Mellen, 1989.

Longacre, Robert E. *Joseph: A Story of Divine Providence: A Text Theoretical and Textlinguistic Analysis of Genesis 37 and 39-48*. Winona Lake, IN: Eisenbrauns, 1989.

Lunn, Nicholas P. "Allusions to the Joseph Narrative in the Synoptic Gospels and Acts: Foundations of a Biblical Type." *JETS* 55.1 (2012): 27-41.

McConville, J. Gordon. "Messianic Interpretation of the Old Testament in Modern Context." Pages 1-17 in *The Lord's Anointed: Interpretation of Old Testament Messianic Texts*. Edited by Philip E. Satterthwaite, Richard S. Hess, and Gordon J. Wenham. Grand Rapids: Baker, 1995.

McGuire, Errol. "The Joseph Story: A Tale of Son and Father." Pages 9-25 in *Images of Man and God: Old Testament Short Stories in Literary Focus*, ed. Burke O. Long. Sheffield: Almond Press, 1981.

Melchin, Kenneth R. "Literary Sources in the Joseph Story." *ScEs* 31 (1979): 93-101.

Milgrom, Jacob. *Leviticus 1-16*. AB 3. New York: Doubleday, 1991.

Miscall, Peter D. "The Jacob and Joseph Stories as Analogies." *JSOT* 6 (1978): 28-40.

Mitchell, David C. "A Dying and Rising Josephite Messiah in *4Q372*." *JSP* 18.3 (2009): 181-205.

_____. "Firstborn *Shor* and *Rem*: A Sacrificial Josephite Messiah in *1 Enoch* 90.37-38 and Deuteronomy 33.17." *JSP* 15.3 (2006): 211-28.

_____. *Messiah ben Joseph*. Newton Mearns, Scotland: Campbell Publications, 2016.

_____. "Messiah bar Ephraim in the Targums." *AS* 4.2 (2006): 221-41.

_____. "Messiah ben Joseph: A Sacrifice of Atonement for Israel." *RRJ* 10.1 (2007): 77-94.

_____. "Rabbi Dosa and the Rabbis Differ: Messiah Ben Joseph in the Babylonian Talmud." *RRJ* 8.1 (2005): 77-90.

Morgenstern, Julian. "The Divine Triad in Biblical Mythology." *JBL* 64 (1945): 15-37.

Morris, Henry Madison. *The Genesis Record: A Scientific and Devotional Commentary on the Book of Beginnings*. Grand Rapids: Baker, 1976.

Morton, J.F. "The Doctrine of the Two Messiahs Among the Jews." *Baptist Review* 9 (1881): 64-73.

Neufeld, Ernest. "The Anatomy of the Joseph Cycle." *JBQ* 22 (1994): 38-46.

Neusner, Jacob. *Introduction to Rabbinic Literature*. New York: Doubleday, 1994.

_____, William S. Green, and Ernest Frerichs, eds. *Judaisms and Their Messiahs at the Turn of the Christian Era*. New York: Cambridge University Press, 1987.

Niccacci, Alviero. "Analysing Biblical Poetry." *JSOT* 74 (1997): 77-93.

Nickelsburg, George W. E. *Resurrection, Immortality, and Eternal Life in Intertestamental Judaism and Early Christianity*. HTS 56. Cambridge: Harvard University Press, 2006.

Obbard, Aug. N. *The Prophecy of Jacob: Notes Critical and Exegetical on Genesis XLIX*. Cambridge: Deighton, Bell, and Co., 1877.

Odom, Robert Leo. *Israel's Preexistent Messiah*. Bronx, NY: Israelite Heritage Institute, 1985.

O'Neill, J.C. "The Lamb of God in the Testament of the Twelve Patriarchs." *JSNT* 2 (1979): 2-30.

Patterson, Richard D. "Joseph, Trusted Favorite." *Fundamentalist Journal* 5 (1986): 24-25.

Pehlke, Helmuth. "An Exegetical and Theological Study of Genesis 49:1-28." PhD diss., Dallas Theological Seminary, 1985.

Peters, J.P. "Jacob's Blessing." *JSBLE* 6.1 (June 1886): 99-116.

Petersen, David L. *Zechariah 9-14 and Malachi: A Commentary*. OTL. Louisville: Westminster John Knox, 1995.

Petrie, George L. *Jacob's Sons*. New York and Washington: Neale Publishing Company, 1910.

Philonenko, Marc. "Joseph and Asenath." *EncJud* 11:418.

Phinney, Brent Lee. "The Relationship of Genesis 49 to the Future of Israel." MA thesis, Dallas Theological Seminary, 1973.

Pick, B. "Old Testament Passages Messianically Applied by the Ancient Synagogue, Part 1." *Hebraica* 2 (1885): 24-32.

_____. "Old Testament Passages Messianically Applied by the Ancient Synagogue, Part 2." *Hebraica* 2 (1886): 129-39.

_____. "Old Testament Passages Messianically Applied by the Ancient Synagogue, Part 3." *Hebraica* 3 (1886): 30-38.

_____. "Old Testament Passages Messianically Applied by the Ancient Synagogue, Part 4." *Hebraica* 3 (1887): 265-68.

_____. "Old Testament Passages Messianically Applied by the Ancient Synagogue, Part 5." *Hebraica* 4 (1887): 46-51.

_____. "Old Testament Passages Messianically Applied by the Ancient Synagogue, Part 6." *Hebraica* 4 (1888): 176-85.

_____. "Old Testament Passages Messianically Applied by the Ancient Synagogue, Part 7." *Hebraica* 4 (1888): 247-49.

Plaut, W. Gunther. *The Torah, A Modern Commentary: Genesis*. New York: Union of American Hebrew Congregations, 1981.

Pomykala, Kenneth E. "Messianism." Pages 938-42 in *The Eerdmans Dictionary of Early Judaism*. Edited by John J. Collins and Daniel C. Harlow. Grand Rapids: Eerdmans, 2010.

Prewitt, Terry J. "Kinship Structures and the Genesis Genealogies." *JNES* 40.2 (April 1981): 87-98.

Rand, Herbert. "Judah and Joseph: A Study in Contrasts." *JBQ* 21 (1993): 127-28.

Reardon, Patrick. "The Joseph Story: Narrative, Theology, & the Christian Hope." *Touchstone* 9 (1996): 26-30.

Rendsburg, Gary A. "Critical Notes: Janus Parallelism in Gen 49:26." *JBL* 99 (1980): 291-93.

_____. "Israelian Hebrew Features in Genesis 49." *MAARAV* 8 (1992): 161-70.

Rösel, Martin. "Die Interpretation von Genesis 49 in der Septuaginta." *BN* 79 (1995): 54-70.

Rodríguez, Ángel Manuel. "Leviticus 16: Its Literary Structure." *AUSS* 34.2 (1996): 269-86.

Rosen, Moishe. *Y'shua: The Jewish Way to Say Jesus.* Chicago: Moody, 1982.

Rosenberg, A. J. "The Complete Tanach with Rashi—Judaica Press." Chabad.org. http://www.chabad.org/library/bible_cdo/aid/63255/jewish/The-Bible-with-Rashi.htm.

Rowley, Harold Henry. *The Servant of the Lord and Other Essays on the Old Testament.* London: Lutterworth, 1952.

Russell, D.S. *The Method and Message of Jewish Apocalyptic.* 1976 ed. OTL. Edited by G. Ernest Wright. Philadelphia: Westminster, 1964.

Ryle, Herbert E. *The Book of Genesis.* Cambridge: Cambridge University Press, 1921.

Sa'adya Gaon. *The Book of Beliefs and Opinions: Translated from the Arabic and the Hebrew by Samuel Rosenblatt.* YJS 1. New Haven: Yale University Press, 1948.

Sailhamer, John H. *Introduction to Old Testament Theology: A Canonical Approach.* Grand Rapids: Zondervan, 1995.

_____. "The Canonical Approach to the OT: Its Effect on Understanding Prophecy." *JETS* 30 (1987): 307-15.

_____. *The Meaning of the Pentateuch: Revelation, Composition and Interpretation.* Downer Grove, IL: InterVarsity Press, 2009.

_____. *The Pentateuch as Narrative: A Biblical-Theological Commentary.* Library of Biblical Interpretation. Grand Rapids: Zondervan, 1992.

Salo, Vello. "Kleinere Beiträge: Joseph, Sohn der Farse." *BZ* 12 (1968): 94-95.

Sanders, James A. "Introduction: Why the Pseudepigrapha?" Pages 13-19 in vol.14 of *The Pseudepigrapha and Early Biblical Interpretation.* Edited by James H. Charlesworth and Craig A. Evans. Sheffield: JSOT Press, 1993.

Sarachek, Joseph. *The Doctrine of the Messiah in Medieval Jewish Literature.* New York: Hermon Press, 1968.

Sarna, Nahum M. *Genesis.* The JPS Torah Commentary. Philadelphia: Jewish Publication Society, 1989.

_____. "Joseph." *EncJud* 11:406-10.

Satterthwaite, Philip E., Richard S. Hess, and Gordon J. Wenham, eds. *The Lord's Anointed: Interpretation of Old Testament Messianic Texts.* Grand Rapids: Baker, 1995.

Schimmel, Sol. "Joseph and His Brothers: A Paradigm for Repentance." *Judaism* 37 (1988): 60-65.

Scholem, Gershom. *The Messianic Idea in Judaism*. New York: Schocken Books, 1971.

Scullion, John J. "The God of the Patriarchs." *Pacifica* 1 (1988): 141-56.

Shea, William H. "Literary Form and Theological Function in Leviticus." Pages 131-68 in *70 Weeks, Leviticus, Nature of Prophecy*. Edited by Frank B. Holbrook. DARCOM 3. Washington, DC: Biblical Research Institute, General Conference of Seventh-day Adventists, 1986.

Sheridan, Mark, ed. *Genesis 12-50*. ACCSOT 2. Downers Grove, IL: InterVarsity Press, 2002.

Sigvartsen, Jan A. "The Afterlife Views and the Use of the Tanakh in Support of the Resurrection Concept in the Literature of Second Temple Period Judaism: The Apocrypha and the Pseudepigrapha." PhD diss., Andrews University, 2006.

Soderlund, Sven K. "Septuagint." *ISBE* 4:400-409.

Sonne, Isaiah. "Genesis 49:25-26." *JBL* 65 (1946): 303-6.

Speiser, E.A. *Genesis*. 3rd ed. AB 1. Garden City, NY: Doubleday, 1987.

Stuart, Douglas. *Old Testament Exegesis: A Primer for Students and Pastors*. Philadelphia: Westminster, 1984.

Sykes, David K. "Patterns in Genesis." PhD diss., Yeshiva University, 1985.

Syren, Roger. *The Forsaken First-Born: A Study of a Recurrent Motif in the Patriarchal Narratives*. JSOTSup 133. Sheffield: JSOT Press, 1993.

Turner, Laurence A. *Announcements of Plot in Genesis*. JSOTSup 96. Sheffield: Sheffield Academic Press, 1990.

Van der Merwe, B. J. "Joseph as Successor of Jacob." Pages 221-32 in *Studia Biblica et Semitica: Theodoro Christiano Vriezen dedicata*. Edited by Theodoro C. Vriezen. Wageningen: Veenman, 1966.

VanGemeren, Willem A., ed. *New International Dictionary of Old Testament Theology and Exegesis*. 5 vols. Grand Rapids: Zondervan, 1997.

Vaticana, Vatican. Biblotheca Apostolica. *The Palestinian Targum to the Pentateuch: Codex Vatican (Neofiti 1)*. Vol. 1. Jerusalem: Makor, 1970.

Viviano, Pauline A. "Methodology, Chronology, Scribes and Inspiration." *Biblical Research* 35 (1990): 51-57.

Von Seebass, Horst. "Die Stammespruche Gen 49:3-27." *ZAW* 96 (1984): 333-50.

Walton, John H. *Chronological and Background Charts of the Old Testament*. Grand Rapids: Zondervan, 1994.

Warning, Wilfried. *Literary Artistry in Leviticus*. BibInt 35. Leiden: Brill, 1999.

Wenham, Gordon J. *Genesis 1-15*. WBC 1. Dallas: Word, 1994.

_____. *Genesis 16-50*. WBC 2. Dallas: Word, 1994.

Westermann, Claus. *Genesis 37-50: A Commentary*. CC. Translated by John Scullion. Minneapolis: Augsburgh, 1986.

Whitehouse, Cope. "The Bahr Jusuf and the Prophecy of Jacob." *PSBA* 8 (November 3 1885): 6-27.

_____. "The Following Communication Has been received from Mr. Cope Whitehouse." *PSBA* 8 (December 1 1885): 57-58.

Whitelaw, Thomas. *Genesis and Exodus*. Pulpit Commentary 1. Grand Rapids: Eerdmans, 1977.

Whybray, R.N. "The Joseph Story and Pentateuchal Criticism." *VT* 18 (1968): 522-28.

Williams, James G. "The Beautiful and the Barren: Conventions in Biblical Type-Scenes." *JSOT* 17 (1980): 107-19.

_____. "Number Symbolism and Joseph as a Symbol of Completion." *JBL* 98 (1979): 86-87.

Wilson, Marvin R. *Our Father Abraham*. Grand Rapids: Eerdmans, 1989.

Wood, Bryant G. "The Sons of Jacob: New Evidence for the Presence of the Israelites in Egypt." *Bible and Spade* 10.2/3 (1997): 53-65.

Wright, Chris. *Knowing Jesus Through the Old Testament*. Downers Grove, IL: InterVarsity Press, 1992.

Zornberg, Avivah Gottlieb. *Genesis: The Beginning of Desire*. Philadelphia: Jewish Publication Society of America, 1995.

INDEX OF REFERENCES

HEBREW BIBLE/
OLD TESTAMENT
Genesis
1–11	57
1:2	68
2:17	58
3:2-5	58
3:15	2, 58, 78, 79, 89, 90
3:16	68
3:17-19	68
3:19b	58
3:23-24	58
11:30	76
12–50	57
12:1-3	70, 73-74, 86, 89
12:2, 3	68
13:16	68
18:8f	68
22	59
25:21	76
27:4	65
27:29	68
28:13-15	68
28:18-22	49
29:3	76
35:1-15	49
37:2	87
37:3	87
37:5-11	87
37:5-8, 10	77
37:7, 9	78
38:9, 27-30	78
40:12-22	87
41:16-20	87
41:41-44, 56	87
41:45	19, 86
41:46-49	20
41:50-52	20
41:53-54	20
41:57	86
42:6	78
43:26	78
44:14	78
45:5-8	6
45:26-46:7	20
47:27	20, 77
47:28	77
47:29	75
48	76
48:2-4	76
48:5	75
48:5, 12	77
48:7	76
48:12	85
48:13-20	75
48:15	49, 76
48:16a	76
48:21f	76
48:22	75
49	1, 2, 3, 4, 10, 23, 35, 42, 43, 51, 53, 56, 64, 92
49:1-27	56, 75
49:1	11, 60, 77-78
49:1-2	10
49:3, 4	75
49:8-11	73
49:8-12	1, 89, 90
49:10	74
49:22-26	1, 4, 15, 46, 75, 85, 89

49:22	6, 43, 47, 64, 65
49:22a	47
49:23	48, 65, 65
49:23f	64
49:24	35, 48
49:24a	66
49:24c	15
49:24d	64
49:24f	64
49:25-26	68
49:25-26a	50
49:25f	64
49:26a	50
49:26b	51
49:26d	69
50	77
50:5	65
50:15	65
50:18	78
50:18, 21	77
50:22	77
50:22, 26	77
50:23	77
50:25	6

Exodus

1-15	57
1:8	6,
12	59
13:19	6
15:1-17	56
15:6	47
17	38
17:9	38
19:6	70
29:6	69
39:30	69

Leviticus

1-7	58
8-10	58
8:9	69
11-15	58
16	57, 59
16:16-19	57
16:20a	57
17-20	57
21-23	57
23	59
24-27	58

Numbers

6:2	51, 69
6:4, 5, 7, 8, 12, 13	69
23:7-10, 18-24	56
24:3-9, 15-24	56
24:14	60
24:15-19	89
26	70

Deuteronomy

4	98
4:3	61
18:15-16	62
18:15	89
21:15-17	75, 76
27-28	98
27-30	58
27:12	6
31:29	60
32-33	56, 89
33	4, 43
33:13-17	69, 85
33:13	6
33:16	51
33:17	23, 24, 51
34:5-12	62

Joshua

1:1-9	62
24:32	6

Judges

1:22, 23, 35	6

9	70
13:2	76
13:5, 7, 13	51
13:5	69
16:17	51

1 Samuel
1:5	76

2 Samuel
1:10	69
19:21	6

1 Kings
2:1	75
11:28	6
12:25	75
22:11	70

2 Kings
11:12	69

Isaiah
8:13-17	49
8:14	68
11:13	34
24:18	34
28:6	49
28:16	68
40:11	49
44:28	62
45:1	62
52-53	43
52:13-53:12	18, 23
53	79, 87

Jeremiah
9:3, 8	48
17:8	47
31:30-34	99

Ezekiel
37:16, 19	6
47:13	6
48:32	6

Amos
2:1	69
5:6	6
5:15	6
6:6	6

Obadiah
18	6

Zechariah
2:3	25
9:9	24
10:6	6
12	23, 25, 38, 43
12-13	36
12:8	36
12:9 ff.	18
12:10	25, 26, 35, 36, 37, 38
12:10, 12	32
12:10-12	38
12:11	38
12:12	24
13:7	36
14:9	36

Malachi
3:1	34, 36, 37
4:1-6	62

Psalms
1	62
1:3	47
2	62
2:7	40
2:7, 8	25
21:5	25
23:1	49, 67

55:4	65	NEW TESTAMENT	
64:3	48	*Matthew*	
78:67	6	1-4	99
80:1	49, 67	4:6	49
80:16	37	5-7	99
80:18	36, 37	7:11	88
81:5-6	6,	21:42-46	49
89:40	69	23:38	98
92:10	47	24:21, 22	88
93:3	47	28:18-20	88
94:3	47		
105:16-22	6,	*Luke*	
105:17-23	67	1:7	76
118:22	49	11:13	88
132:18	69		
147:2	38	*John*	
		1:14	87
Proverbs		1:29, 36	16
25:18	48	3:16	87
		11:49-50	19
Lamentations		11:51-52	19
4:7	51		
		Acts	
Job		2:38	88
16:9	65	3:18-26	62
30:21	65	7:37	62
Ecclesiastes		*Romans*	
1:2	47	5:8	87
12:11	67	8:22-25	88
		8:35-39	88
Daniel			
2:34, 35, 45	49	*Galatians*	
8:4	70	3:29	99
		5:22	88
1 Chronicle		6:16	99
5:1-2	6, 75		
5:1	76	*Ephesians*	
36	62	1:5	88
		2:14-18	99
2 Chronicle		2:20	49
18:10	70	5:30	99

Philippians
2:6-12   84

Hebrews
4:15   87
8-10   89

1 Peter
2:4-10   49

Revelation
1-2   89
7:3   88
11:15   85, 87
12:5   85
13:11-18   88
14:6-12   88
19:16   85
20:6   88
21-22   87
21:1-5   88

APOCRYPHA/
PSEUDEPIGRAPHA
1 Maccabees
14:41   27

2 Maccabees
7   16

4 Ezra
7.28-29   23

1 Enoch
90:37-38   23

3 Enoch
45:5   22

Sibylline Oracles
5.256-59   23

Testament of the Twelve Patriarchs

T. Naphtali
5:1-8   23

T. Joseph
19:8.11   15

T. Benjamin
3:1-4:1   15
3:8   14, 15, 17, 18

T. Moses
9:7-10:3   16

Joseph and Aseneth
1:3-6   20
5:2   21
5:5   20
6:2-6   21
11:2   21
14:1   21
14:9   21
15:7   21
16:16   21
17:8   21
18   21
18:11   21
19:5   21
19:10-11   21
23:10   21
28:13   21
29:8-9   20

4 Maccabees
9-18   16

Index of References

QUMRAN/
DEAD SEA SCROLLS
4Q175 [4QTest]	5, 23, 26
4Q372	23
4Q474	23
4QMessAp	23
11QMelech	23

TARGUMIC TEXTS
Targum Pseudo-Jonathan
Genesis
41:45	20

Exodus
1:15	17
7:11	17
40:9-11	4
40:11	8, 29

Numbers
22:22	17

Targum Song of Songs
4:5	4, 8
7:4	4

RABBINIC LITERATURE
'Aggadat Berešit
63	29
70	29
79	29

'Aggadat Mashiah	31
20-24	29

Asereth Melakhim	31

Asereth Otot	31

Babylonian Talmud
Sukkah	24
52a	8, 25, 35
52b	25

Genesis Rabbah
75:5	24
75.6	4, 29
99.2	4, 29

Kitab 'al-'amanat wal-I'tiqadat 31

Kuntres Acharon §20 to Yalqut
Shimoni on Pentateuch   29

Midrash Aleph Beth
11b.15	4

Midrash Vayosha
Exod 15:18	31

Midrash Tanḥuma
11b.1-15	29
11.3 [1.103a]	4-5, 29

Mishnah
Sotah 1.9	41

Nistarot Rav Shimon ben Yoḥai 31
12	29

Number Rabbah
14.1	5, 29

Otot haMasiah	31
5.7-8	29
6.11-12	29

Otot Rav Shimon ben Yoḥai   31

Pirqe Mash	31
5.45	29
Pirqei Hekhalot Rabbati	
§38-40	31
Pirqe Rabbi Eliezer	
22a.ii	29
Pesiqta de Rab Kahana	
5.9	5
Pesiqta Rabbati	
8.4	5, 29
15.14/15	5
33.6	29
34.36-37	4
36-37	29
36	29
36.1	29
36.2	30
37	29
37.1-3	30
Sefer Zerubbabel	31
50	29
Sefer Zohar	
Mishpatim	
478	29
479	29
Song of Songs Rabbah	
2.13.4	5
Tefillat Rav Shimon ben Yoḥai	
	29, 31

Tosefta Targum	
Zech 12:10	4, 8, 29
Yalquṭ Shimoni	
§570 on Zech 4:3	29

INDEX OF AUTHORS

Aberbach, Moses 41
Alexander, P. 22
Alexander, T. D. 77, 78
Alter, R. 48-49
Ambrose of Milan 5
Aptowitzer, V. 20
Bacharach, Naphtali ben Jacob Elchanan 40
Baron, D. 39, 40
Battenfield, J. R. 46
Ben Meir 50, 51
Blenkinsopp, J. 74
Blidstein, G. J. 8
Braude, W. G. 29, 30
Brenton, L. C. L. 66
Burchard, C. 17, 19, 20, 21
Charlesworth, J. H. 9, 10, 11
Cross, Jr., F. M. 4
Cyprian 41
Davidson, R. M. 2, 59, 62, 80, 87, 88, 92, 100-106
de Jonge, M. 10, 16, 23, 24
Deane, W. J. 42
Delitzsch, F. 66
Dix, G. H. 17, 18, 19
Douglas, R. C. 19
Doukhan, J. 8, 68, 79, 89
Driver, S. R. 68
Dykers, P. 9
Elgvin, T. 23
Ephrem the Syrian 5
Evans, C. A. 9, 16, 27
Fairbairn, P. 82
Flusser, D. 27
Freedman, D. N. 4
Fritsch, C. 9, 67, 86, 90

Gevirtz, S. 43, 76, 77
Glenny, W. E. 2
Gordon, C. H. 50
Gugliotto, L. J. 24
Hale, J. G. 49
Hamelek, E. 40
Hamilton, V. P. 66, 69, 89
Harris, R. L. 61
Heal, K. S. 5, 97
Heard, W. J. 16
Heck, J. 4, 43
Heineman, J. 8, 24, 79
Henry, P. 41
Herr, M. D. 28-29
Hill, A. E. 61
Himmelfarb, M. 8, 23, 31
Hippolytus 5
Hollander, H. W. 10, 11, 16, 41
Holtz, T. 19, 27
Ibn Ezra 35, 36, 37, 39
Irenaeus 42
Isaac ben Judah Abravanel 39
Jones, A. 86
Jukes, A. 82
Kaiser, Jr., W. C. 89
Kee, H. C. 10, 11, 16
Keil, C. F. 66
Kidner, D. 67
Kimhi, D 37
Klausner, J. 25
Knohl, I. 16
Koch, K. 16
Kugel, J. L. 41
Liver, J. 11, 13, 79
Lockshine, M. I. 47, 50, 51
Longacre, R. E. 53, 54, 55, 56

Lunn, N. P. 5
McGuire, E. 83, 84
Milgrom, J. 63
Mitchell, D. C. 5, 8, 23, 26, 29, 31, 32, 36, 37, 38, 39
Morton, J. 4, 40
Moses Aberbach 41
Moses Alshech 39
Moses ben Nahman 37
Moshe ben Shem-Tov 38
Moses de León 38
Nachmanides 37
Nichol, F. D. 67
O'Neill, J. C. 16, 17
Pehlke, H. 46
Philonenko, M. 19
Pomykala, K. E. 27
Radak 37
Ramban 37, 38
Rashban 47
Rashi 34, 35, 37
Reardon, P. 41, 42, 94
Rendsburg, G. A. 50, 51
Rodríguez, Á. 58
Rösel, M. 46
Rosenberg, A. J. 34
Rufinus of Aquileia 5
Ryle, H. E. 49
Sa'adya Gaon 33, 34
Sailhamer, J. H. 56, 57, 61, 62
Sanders, J. A. 9
Sarachek, J. 38
Sarna, N. M. 6, 49, 53, 64, 65
Shea, W. H. 57
Sheridan, M. 5
Shlomo Yitzchaki 34
Sigvartsen, J. A. 12
Soderlund, S. K. 7
Speiser, E. A. 48
Syren, R. 76
Tertullian 41
Turner, L. A. 73, 85

Van der Merwe, B. J. 69, 75, 76, 77
Walton, J. H. 52, 72
Warning, W. 58
Wenham, G. J. 48, 66, 68, 69, 89
Whitehouse, C. 43
Whitelaw, T. 87
Williams, J. 76, 77
Wilson, M. R. 68

SUBJECT INDEX

A

Abraham, 1, 6, 50, 54, 75, 77–78, 86
　blessing, 79
　covenant, 1, 64
　promises, 49, 73, 78
Adam, 22, 30, 54, 78, 100–101, 103
Ancient Yahwistic Poetry, 4
Antitype, 81–82, 100–105
Antitypical
　fulfillment, 82, 88
　Joseph, 66, 82, 85, 87
Apocalyptic midrashim, 29, 31–34
Apocrypha, 16

B

Bar Kokhba, 24
　period, 24
　revolt, 8, 22, 26
Biblical literature, 56
Biblical type(s), 5, 99–100
Biblical typology, 81
　basic elements of, 81
　Christological-soteriological element of, 81
　ecclesiological element of, 81
　eschatological element of, 81
　historical element of, 81
　prophetic element of, 81
　substructure of, 100–101, 106
Blessing(s), 1, 4, 23, 42–44, 47, 50–52, 64, 66, 68–69, 73–77, 79, 83, 86, 88, 98
　Abrahamic, 79
　be a, 74, 77
　Divine blessing, 69
　from his father, 69
　Joseph, 75
　Joseph's comprehensive, 64
　of firstborn, 76
　of Joseph, 50, 63, 76
　of many children, 68
　to his father, 68

C

Christ, 2, 5, 42, 81, 90, 92, 97, 99, 101–2
　Jesus, 15, 17, 44, 62, 82, 85, 89, 99
Christian Interpolations, 15, 19
Christians, 5–6, 8–10, 16–17, 22, 40, 85, 87–90, 98–99, 101
Christological, 41, 80–81, 95, 97, 100–101, 106
Church, 81, 88, 99, 101–2
Covenant, 2, 14, 37, 98–99
　Abrahamic, 1, 64
　Ark of the, 41, 62
　at Sinai, 106
　blessings, 98
　curses, 58, 98
　new, 106

D

David, 40, 100, 105
　antitypical, 105
　family of, 24
　house of, 35
　king, 75
　messiah ben/son of, 22–23, 25, 27, 31, 33–34, 36–40, 73, 79
　new, 105

son of, 79
Davidic
  king, 89
  kingdom, 70
  rulership, 70
Dead Sea Scrolls, 5, 7, 10, 16, 27
Descendant(s), 1, 15, 18, 49, 56, 69–70, 78
Doctrine, 4, 8, 13, 17, 38
Doctrine of the two anointed figures, 13

E

Early Christian Period, 41
Early Christians, 17
Early Church, 44, 92
Early Church Fathers, 7, 41–42, 44, 94
Early Jewish Interpretation, 7, 40
Early Judaism, 9
Ecclesiological, 80–81, 88, 100–101, 106
Egypt, 1, 6, 20–21, 43, 50, 54, 68, 86–87, 99
Ephraim, 32, 43, 65, 70, 72, 75
  and Manasseh, 6, 65, 70, 76
  house of, 37
  our true Messiah, 30, 37
  tribe of, 40, 70
  twin tribes, 6
Esau, 24, 54, 76
Eschatological, 1, 22, 27, 31, 59, 61, 80–81, 92, 99, 101
  age, 2, 82
  aspect(s), 3, 63, 80, 87–88
  climax, 59
  consummated, 88
  frame(work), 62
  fulfillment, 2-3, 81, 87-89, 99-101
  hermeneutic of biblical typology, 80, 102, 105
  implications, 3, 64
  Joseph, 66, 72, 87, 92
  messianic emphasis, 62
  messianic figures, 88
  sequence, 27
  shepherd, 68
  substructure, 100–101
Eschatology, 98
  appropriated, 88, 99, 101
  consummated, 88, 99, 101
  inaugurated, 88, 99, 101
Event(s), historical, 8, 44, 100, 106

G

Genealogies, 4, 57, 73

H

Hebrew Bible, 7, 53, 104
Hebrew Scripture, 3, 5–9, 21, 25, 41, 46–47, 51, 53, 90
History, 4, 22, 61, 70, 78, 81, 98–99
  of interpretation, 2, 4–6, 9, 92
  primeval, 68
  salvation, 59, 80
  spiritual, 9

I

Inaugurated eschatology, 88, 99, 101
Interpretation, 7, 15, 18, 36, 38, 47–49, 58, 67, 69
  Christological, 97
  dual, 68
  early Jewish, 7, 40
  history of, 2, 4–6, 92
  in early Christian texts, 5
  inner-biblical, 6
  late Jewish, 23
  messianic, 25
  of biblical types, 99
  parenthetical, 68
  predominant, 4
  prevalent, 47

stream of, 4
typological, 100, 103
Isaac, 50, 54, 75–78, 86
Israel, 4, 13–15, 18, 22, 30–32, 37–39, 41, 70, 98–99, 105–106
   deportation of, 75
   enemies, 23
   ethnical, 98
   exiles of, 38
   family, 50
   foundation of, 67
   guilt of, 39
   house of, 38
   /Jacob, 6, 10
   king of, 71
   leaders(hip of), 54, 70
   nation of, 100
   new, 99
   northern, 7, 75
   people of, 7, 99
   shepherd, 50
   sons of, 78
   stone of, 15, 35, 46, 49, 67–68
   survival, 67
   spiritual, 99, 106
   tribes of, 4, 70–71
   typology, 100, 106
Israelite(s), 6–7, 35, 70, 79, 99

J

Jacob, 1, 4, 10, 14, 48–50, 54, 56–57, 65, 68, 73–79, 85–86, 92
   adopted by, 75–76
   appointed first-born of, 77
   blessed, 11
   blessed his sons, 53
   blessing (given) by/of, 44, 75–76
   death, 1, 75, 78
   family, 53–55
   favorite son, 87
   heir, 76
   mighty One of, 35, 46, 67
   last words, 10
   oracles given by, 51
   prediction delivered by, 43
   sons of, 10, 20
   successor, 1, 75, 77
   testament, 68, 78
   vision about Joseph, 3
   words, 1, 65–66
Jerusalem, 32, 38, 106
   come against, 36
   destruction of, 23
   inhabitants/dwellers of, 35–36
   liberate, 31, 33
Jerusalem Targum, 51
Jesus, 17, 39–40, 42, 49, 82, 87–89, 97, 99
   alluding to, 40
   antitypical fulfillment, 82
   antitypical Joseph, 83
   as the fulfillment, 17
   as their Messiah, 17
   belief in, 40
   Christ, see Christ
   comparisons between Joseph and, 87
   figure of, 41
   foreshadowed, 44
   kill, 19
   lamb of God, 17
   life, 2, 44, 84–85
   messianic claim, 49
   resurrection, 41, 97
   suffering and death, 18
   type for, 4–5, 42, 82, 94, 96
   would die, 19
Jewish, 5, 9, 16, 19, 22, 93
   army, 33
   authorship, 10, 16
   apocalypses, 8
   belief, 2, 4, 15, 44, 92
   -Christian polemics, 8
   context, 2, 80, 82, 92

documents, 10
diaspora, 7
interpretation, 7, 23, 40
literature, 47
mysticism, 38
origin, 10, 27
people, 44, 98
scriptures, 17, 19, 43
thought, 16, 24, 68
tradition, 2, 9, 16, 26, 41–42, 67, 79, 88
writing(s), 5, 17–18, 23
Jews, 5, 8–9, 15, 17, 19, 33, 87, 89, 98
Joseph, 2–9, 11–12, 14–15, 19–25, 35, 40–44, 46–54, 56, 64–70, 74–78, 80, 82–83, 85–88, 90, 92, 94–97
  a prototype of Jesus Christ, 17
  blessing, 1, 17, 35, 43, 75
  bones, 6, 14, 41
  brothers, 20, 54, 65, 77
  darkest hour, 54
  descendants, 69
  descended from, 33–34
  dreams, 85
  enemies, 48
  exaltation, 67
  -Jesus interpretation, 5
  life, 42, 76, 82–83, 92
  love story, 19
  messiah ben, see Messiah ben Joseph
  narrative, 2–3, 5–6, 10, 20, 44, 49, 53–54, 56–57, 82–84, 86, 89, 93, 97
  oracle, 3–4, 7, 46, 51, 56, 64–65, 67, 72, 80, 82–84, 88–89, 92
  patriarch, 17
  rulership, 14
  story, 42, 53, 55–56, 97
  tradition (Messiah ben Joseph), 5, 24, 38

  tribes, 64, 69–70, 72
Joshua, 6, 38, 70–71, 100, 104
Judah, 1, 12, 15–16, 34, 43, 52, 56, 72–75, 78–79, 89
  adversary of, 34
  and Joseph, 1, 3, 15, 54, 56, 64, 73–74, 78–79, 88
  blessing(s), 1, 4, 74
  descendants of, 78
  Ephraim and, 70
  leadership, 1, 73
  line of, 73
  not envy, 34
  Levi and, 11, 13, 15, 18, 42, 88, 92
  Messiah ben, 39, 79, 89
  Messiah from, 42
  oracle(s), 73–74
  preeminence of, 54
  promises given to, 90
  Royal Messiah, 92
  supremacy of Judah, 78
  tribe of, 17
Judaism, 6, 16, 98
  early, 9
  later, 9
  pre-Christian, 16
  rabbinic, 5, 23–24
  Second Temple period, 9, 98

K

Kingdom prophecies, 98–99, 101

L

Lamb of God, 14–17, 42
Land, promised, 1, 6, 58, 70
Levi, 11–13, 15–16, 18, 42, 52, 88–90, 92
Lord's Anointed, 77
LXX (Septuagint), 7, 48, 50, 58, 66, 89

M

Manasseh, 6, 65, 72, 75–76
Medieval Jewish Literature, 33, 39
Messiah, 1, 15, 17–18, 22–24, 27, 29–31, 38, 40, 42, 49, 58, 62, 67, 79–80, 82, 85, 87, 89–90, 92, 98, 104–5
 antitypical, 86
 ben David, 23, 26-27, 31–34, 36–38, 40, 73, 79
 ben/bar Ephraim, 4, 8, 31, 33, 36
 ben Joseph, 2, 4–5, 8, 17–18, 22–27, 29, 31–40, 43–44, 73, 79, 82, 89, 92
 ben Levi, 18, 73, 79, 89
 coming, 42, 49, 62, 64, 67–68, 72, 79, 82, 86, 88, 92
 Ephraim, 4, 29, 31, 33
 Josephite, 5, 26
 king, 24, 29, 31, 59
 ministry, 89, 92
 one, 16
 royal, 11, 89, 92
 son of David, 79
 son of Joseph, 8, 67
 suffering, 2, 18, 40, 44, 79
 suffering and militant, 8
 three/threefold, 79, 88–89
 type of the New Testament, 2
 two/dual, 8, 11, 17, 34
Messianic, 39, 61, 64, 78, 89, 92, 103
 age, 23, 43–44
 and eschatological implications, 3, 64
 aspect(s), 1, 3, 64, 80, 89, 93
 figures, 11, 16, 27, 34, 88
 interpretation, 25
 king(dom), 13, 27, 61, 98
 passages, 3, 89
 promise, 2
 prophecy/ies, 1, 67, 89, 90, 98
 type(s), 1, 89
Midrash(im), 8, 27–29, 31–32

Moses, 4, 16, 38, 41, 44, 62, 69–70, 100, 104
 narrative, 57, 60
MT (Masoretic Text), 7, 50, 58, 99

N

Narrative, 4, 6, 11–12, 27, 33, 54, 56–57, 60–61, 75–76, 78, 85–86, 97, 99
 Exodus, 57, 60, 99
 Joseph, 2–3, 5–6, 10, 20, 44, 49, 53–54, 56–57, 82–84, 86, 89, 93, 97
 Moses, 57, 60
 Patriarchal, 57, 60
 -Poetry-Epilogue pattern, 57
 Wilderness, 57, 60
New Testament, 9, 62, 88, 90, 98, 100
 antitype, 81, 101
 fulfillment, 81
 messiah, 2
 salvation history, 80
 writers, 7, 49

O

Old Testament, 9, 17, 27, 65, 80–81, 98–103
 heroes, 9
 indicator, 82
 prophecies, 98
 source, 7
 types, 81–82, 87, 94, 100–105
Oracle, Joseph, 3–4, 7, 46, 51, 56, 64–65, 67, 72, 80, 82–84, 88–89, 92
Oracles, 3, 51–52, 72, 74, 79, 85, 92

P

Patriarchal Narratives, 57, 60
Patriarch(s), 11, 17, 30–31, 50, 74, 76–77
Pentateuch, 3, 6, 8, 56–58, 60–62, 89,

99
Priesthood, 13, 27, 90, 100, 106
Promise(s), 59, 68–69, 74, 77–78, 86, 89
Prophecy/-ies, 1, 3, 14, 18, 27, 36-39, 41, 43-44, 49, 57, 62, 80, 85, 89, 98-99, 101
   classical, 101
   fulfilled, 62
   heavenly, 14, 17
   messianic, 1, 67, 89
   mother, 89
   of the coming Messiah, 50
   unfulfilled, 73
   Zechariah, 19, 36, 39
Prophet Elijah, 33
Prophet(s), 27, 41, 62, 94–95, 98–100, 106
Pseudepigrapha, 9, 16, 19

R

Rabbinic, 2, 8
   genre, 27
   Judaism, 5, 23–24, 43
   literature/writings, 2, 23
Rachel, 50, 53, 76
Rebekah, 50, 76. 86
Royal Joseph, 69

S

Sarah, 50, 76
Scripture(s), 18, 29–30, 42, 65–66, 68, 75, 79, 83–84, 87–89, 92
Second Temple Period, 2, 5, 9, 23, 26–27, 41, 75, 98–99
Septuagint, see LXX
Story, Joseph, 42, 53, 55–56, 97
Suffering, 8, 18, 29–30, 42, 65–66, 68, 74, 79, 83, 87–88, 92
   and militant Messiah, 8
   Joseph, 65–66, 89

Messiah, 2, 40, 44, 79
Messiah ben Joseph, 18
savior, 16, 44
servant, 2, 16, 18
Symbol(ism), 21, 41, 49, 51–52, 97

T

TaNaKh, 6–7, 34, 59, 62, 99
Targum Onkelos, 50, 89
Targum Pseudo-Jonathan, 50, 89
Testament, 10–11, 18, 64, 68, 78
Testament of the Twelve Patriarchs, 9–15, 42
Threefold Eschatological Aspect, 87–88
Threefold Messiah, 88–89
Tribe(s), 42–43, 56, 64–65, 70, 72, 74, 79
   attributes of the, 64
   Joseph, 64, 70, 72, 75
   of Ephraim, 40, 70
   of Israel, 4, 71
   of Joseph, 39, 43, 48, 69–70, 72
   of Judah, 17
   of Levi, 70
   of Levi and Judah, 15
   of Manasseh and Ephraim, 70
   ten northern, 70
   twelve, 70–71
   twin, 6
Type, 80, 82, 87, 92, 98, 100
   antitype, 5, 81, 100
   biblical, 99-100
   messianic, 1, 89
   of a coming eschatological Joseph, 67
   of/for Jesus (Christ), 2, 4–5, 41–42, 44, 82, 92, 94, 96–97
   of Joseph, 88
   of Michael, 21
   of God's Son, 22
   of the coming High Priest, 89

of the coming Messiah, 42, 64, 67, 86, 88
of the eschatological Shepherd and Stone of Israel, 68
  of the future Messiah, 2
  of the Messiah, 82
  of the Messiah's first coming, 89
  of the New Testament Messiah, 2
  of the suffering Messiah, 2
  Old Testament, 2, 81–82, 87, 94, 100–105
  prophetic, 64, 80, 90
  to antitype, 81
Typological, 2, 58, 80–82, 100–101, 103
  aspect, 83, 93
  indicator, 82, 92
  Joseph, 88
  pointer, 92
  redemptive perspective, 58
Typology, 80–81, 101
  Davidson's view of, 2
  elements of biblical, 81
  four different views of, 2
  four-fold substructure of biblical, 100, 106
  in scripture, 92
  Israel, 100, 106
  narrative, 61, 80
  substructure of biblical, 100–101
  verbal indicator of, 103–105

W

War Messiah, 4, 29
Warlike Messiah, 24

www.ingramcontent.com/pod-product-compliance
Lightning Source LLC
Chambersburg PA
CBHW070155100426
42743CB00013B/2919